Thomas R. Kinman

GETTING YOUR FAMILY ON YOUR SIDE

John 5: Pr 114

GETTING YOUR FAMILY ON YOUR SIDE

NEVA COYLE
AND
DAVID DIXON

BETHANY HOUSE PUBLISHERS
MINNEAPOLIS, MINNESOTA 55438
A Division of Bethany Fellowship, Inc.

Published by Bethany House Publishers
A Division of Bethany Fellowship, Inc.
6820 Auto Club Road, Minneapolis, Minnesota 55438

Printed in the United States of America

Library of Congress Cataloging-in-Publication Data
Coyle, Neva, 1943–
    Getting your family on your side.

    1. Reducing—Psychological aspects. 2. Obesity—Patients—Family relationships. 3. Christian life—
1960–   . I. Dixon, David, 1944–   . II. Title.
RM222.2.C66   1987   613.2'5   87–21789
ISBN 0–87123–960–4

DEDICATION

To Families . . .

The families of those who helped us
research this book,

The families of those who will read it,

And affectionately to our own families,
who help us live out these concepts
in our day-to-day lives.

ABOUT THE AUTHORS

NEVA COYLE has a nationwide ministry through Overeaters Victorious, of which she is founder and president. Her recent surgery for reversal of a previous bypass operation and the difficulties of her recovery started the research and writing from which this book was developed. Neva, her husband and teenage son make their home in Redlands, California.

DAVID DIXON, Ph.D., Marriage and Family Therapist, and eating disorder counselor, supervises his Christian counseling practice in Bakersfield, California. His work with those suffering with eating disorders and their families has been important background for this book. He and his wife are parents of two teenage boys and live in Bakersfield.

SPECIAL THANKS

The text of this book is written in a form that infers it is entirely my work. However, that style is used for ease of reading and continuous flow of the material. Dr. Dave Dixon has been an integral part of the writing of this book—from the very inception to the final draft. He has graciously allowed me to work within the limitations of my abilities to communicate by taking a less visible position.

Dave Dixon and I are grateful to our "mentor" and advisor, Bodie Thoene, for her encouragement both through giving us her time unselfishly and through sharing herself and her talent to help build within me the confidence to express myself even more fully in print.

Our editor, Carol Johnson, has been careful to make this book her priority. Thank you, Carol, for your caring way of making yourself so clear. Editing for a writer can be an emotional crisis of no small magnitude, but you have made it an experience that can be faced with certainty of survival.

We also could not have written this book without the people who participated in our surveys and endless questions. It was a painful experience for many and we humbly thank you for sharing with us your pain. We sincerely dedicate this book to you.

CONTENTS

A PERSONAL WORD FROM NEVA COYLE

This is not a weight-loss book. It's more. It will not help you get thin—not *directly*. Rather, it deals with some of the hidden obstacles that may be keeping you from sticking with an effective program of weight loss and long-term maintenance. It is about overeating and how your family can sabotage or support you when it comes to controlling your habit of overeating.

More than ten years ago I founded a Christian organization called Overeaters Victorious. Since then, I have been writing Bible studies for those struggling with being overweight, teaching seminars, leading retreats and counseling individuals on occasion. I have both a *subjective* and an *objective* viewpoint when talking with overweight people, for one simple reason: I am one.

I have poured my heart, and literally my life, into my work since starting Overeaters Victorious. I have a full-time ministry through my writing and speaking, encouraging overweight people all over our country and even beyond. But I have faced battles all along the way: My weight, my health, crises in my life, changes in my family through death, role reversal in my marriage; also constant challenges in my ministry, financial pressures, leadership and administrative responsibilities requiring skills that keep me on the front edge of learning; then the loss of privacy as a public figure, betrayal by close friends, my children growing up and beginning to leave home all brought pain. Added to all that, there has been a constant pressure to be thin!

I won't go into details, but will tell you briefly that some years ago I underwent intestinal bypass surgery in an attempt to lose weight. This surgery was dangerous, wreaked havoc on my health and was less than satisfactory in helping me to permanently lose weight. Even though I stayed within a 1200-cal-per-day limit, and with the surgery's added "assistance"—well, it was still becoming increasingly difficult to keep weight off.

We know now, fifteen years later, that surgery to assist in weight loss has long-term consequences. One side effect is a metabolic slowdown, making it possible for one's body to live on less and less calories and still gain weight. That is what happened to me. In short, the surgery did *not* help me to keep my weight down, and because of the metabolic changes, reversing the operation would make me gain regardless of what I ate. Then, severe gastrointestinal distress and dangerous vitamin shortages in my body left me no choice but to undergo the dreaded reversal. I tried to prepare myself emotionally and spiritually for what would certainly be the most tragic situation I could think of at the time—a weight gain.

I had been warned that recovery would also be difficult, in part, because I was ill going into the procedure. Though I'd learned through experience that pain can also bring deeper understanding into God's Word, His promises of love and care for me, I dreaded what lay ahead. There were many moments of lonely agonizing.

During this high-pressured time, I sought professional counsel to help me sort through the confusion and hurt. That was when I met Dr. Dave Dixon. During my sessions with him, I came to a more balanced approach to life as I confronted many painful emotions. With his help, and the Lord's, I made it through the surgery and the difficult days beyond.

Since then, Dr. Dixon and I have made an unusual transition: Once we were counselor and client; now we are friends.

In this friendship, I became aware of how many overweight people Dr. Dixon sees in his practice. I marveled at his effectiveness as he treated entire families, not just overweight individuals. In his practice, and in my ministry, we discovered that many similar situations arose. We became curious about family relationships and their influence on weight gain and loss. Research followed.

The result is this book, which Dr. Dixon and I have coauthored. We questioned 430 over-weight Christians, most of them women. We found some predictable results—and some sur-prises. As we read the questionnaires filled out by these people, we felt the isolation that most of them expressed; we became aware of the pain in their childhood families. Moreover, we could see the same patterns repeated in their present fam-ilies. Some complicated situations turned up.

For example, one woman reported that her husband wanted her to lose weight; but on the other hand their social life and family activities centered around eating out. As it happens, she has the most difficulty with overeating when they eat out; it's then her husband offers tempting des-serts. More confusion surfaced in their sex life: Her husband says he is "turned off by fat women." She senses that being fat protects her from the advances of other men. So even though she feels less sexy for her husband, she feels safe from temptations outside the marriage.

Another confused woman wrote, saying, "Help me, I am desperate! I am a battered wife. My husband refuses to have sex with me (other than oral sex), because he hates me for being so fat. I feel as trapped as an alcoholic or drug ad-dict—or a prostitute." She also related a history of foster homes where she suffered sexual, verbal and physical abuse as a child. To this day, she is totally rejected by her own mother. Her doctor has suggested stomach-stapling, but her husband refuses. Why? Does he like hating her fat better than he would like loving her thin? She has reached out to her pastor, who told her that all fat people are lazy and guilty of gluttony. All she had to do, he counseled, was to control herself, refuse to eat—to fast.

We wrote to her and recommended that she see a Christian counselor, one who could help her sort through the relationships, past and present, which are helping to keep her a prisoner to being overweight. While this one woman feels alone, she is not. Literally, there are thousands like her. In his practice, Dave has learned that it is not unusual to see a woman in treatment who, after going through a divorce and a total life change, loses weight without much apparent effort. Others lose weight after the death of their spouse.

Much of what we learned corroborated my personal findings. Facing the reversal surgery, I knew I was headed for the most difficult period of discipline, both with food and emotions, and that if I didn't have the full cooperation of my family, I would not only gain weight, but witness the end of my ministry. Scary prospects.

We'd made stabs at family support before, but only in a give-and-take situation. They would put up with my "health food kick" for a while, if I would give in and splurge with them occasionally. Not a verbal agreement, you understand, but an agreement all the same. But in my predicament, there was no room for splurges. I would need the support of my family as never before.

The outcome of the second surgery? Most bypass-reversal patients gain back more than they lost in the first place. Because I do not weigh as much as I did when I had the bypass originally, I am considered a success. Nonetheless, I have gained. When I look in the mirror, I feel like a failure. For me, while weight loss is presently next to impossible; *managing* my weight is victory.

What gets me through? The loving, emotional support of my husband.

Many of the concepts in this book refer to the husband/wife relationship. However, the same principles apply in any deep relationship where there is a commitment or bond—between friends, siblings, parents and even roommates. The illustrations we present occur not only in the family of origin, but also in the present family situation. For those who are single, you may find application with roommates, close friends and church groups. Other books encourage you to look at yourself and your weight problem individually. Here, we are dealing with you and your weight problem within the context of your close relationships. To simplify, these relationships will for the most part be called "the family." Our aim is to show you the impact of these relationships on your weight management process and the impact that process has on them. Ultimately, we will achieve our purpose if, after reading this book, you become aware of the ways in which your family is *not* supportive—and if not, you learn how to find alternative reinforcement for your weight loss program.

With that as our basis, let's begin with some of the most important questions you can ask yourself on the road to a new, freer, happier, slimmer you. . . .

CHAPTER ONE

MAKING THE CONNECTION

W hat would life be like if you were thin? How would things change if you were not an overeater? Would you cook differently? Bake less? Would you put more fruit and vegetables in your shopping cart in place of cookies and soda? Would you choose whole grains over doughy white bread and sweet rolls? Grapes instead of goodies? Cherries in place of chips?

Now ask yourself: How would these changes affect your family?

Let's say you are a woman who wears a size 42 blouse. You are perhaps 125 to 150 pounds overweight. Then let's say you lose that extra weight and within a few months' time you can wear a size 12. Picture the changes that would bring into your whole way of life. A new wardrobe, a new hairstyle and perhaps a little more makeup. You feel more like going out and doing things. You decide to learn to bowl or ski. Maybe you want to ride a bicycle. Finally you feel unashamed in a bathing suit.

These are wonderful positive changes for you. *But are they wonderful and positive for your family?*

Consider: For your husband it would mean budgeting allowances for the new clothes, hairstyles, makeup and bicycle. Even though he may have promised to buy you anything you wanted if you lost weight, suddenly he has to face what will happen to his finances as he makes good on those promises. Maybe attention and praise will come your way—some of it from other men. Is he ready for that? It can mean changes in what you cook and serve to the family. Less pasta and fried foods, no more cakes, pies and cookies. Think of their reaction!

The point is, when a person goes on a diet and loses weight, the entire family is affected. Author, doctor and nutritionist Dr. Cheraskin says, "When you deal with food problems, you are dealing with family problems." Another author, therapist Virginia Satir, says, "If one member of a family has pain which is exhibited in symptoms" (as in the case of overeaters), "all members will, to some degree, react to that pain. They cannot NOT react."[1]

We see this true in cases where, for example, there is an alcoholic in the family. There are complex issues of blame and enablement, also financial stresses caused by lost jobs or irresponsible handling of family finances. When a family member is ill, there is an impact made on the whole family. Perhaps you remember a time when one of your family was in the hospital and the whole family routine had to be adjusted to accommodate the situation.

The same family impact occurs when one is an overeater. The entire family is impacted by the overeating, and again when the overeater takes steps to correct such behavior.

When attempting to change one's eating patterns, habits and food choices, the family process is changed as well. And the one initiating the changes, most likely the mother, can open herself to criticism from her family at a crucial moment when she most needs their support.

I remember the first time I put broccoli on the table. One of my children wrinkled her nose and with a dramatic expression of disgust said, "What is that awful smell?" Another said with equal disdain, "Do *we* have to eat that?" The first child responded, "If we do, I bet I'll throw up."

I looked at my husband, hoping for some reinforcement. He said, with a cool tone, "If it's healthy and good for you, it won't taste good."

It felt like somebody had just torpedoed my boat!

It was quite a while before I tried to serve anything other than peas or corn. I continued cooking *their* preferences for them, along with new, calorie-wise choices for me. Many times, what I was eating was examined, exclaimed over, and often met with a nonverbal evaluation: one hand over the mouth, the index finger and thumb of the other securely closing the nose to shut out the "awful smell."

If you've tried to change your eating habits, perhaps you've heard dampening responses, like the following:

"Why do we have to eat this stuff. Are we out of peanut butter and jelly?"

"Could I have a TV dinner?"

Or this table blessing: "Thank you, Jesus, for our food, help us to be kind and good. And thank God we don't have to eat that junk Mom eats. Amen."

This is not what we want or need from our families. What we need is support. We need them to sacrifice and just try to eat broiled fish once in a while. We need our husbands to get behind us with encouragement instead of a snide remark about the size of our backside.

Is there a connection between the family and our fat? Yes, there is. Is your family involved in your overeating? Probably so. Not just in comments about our dieting efforts but in many other ways as well. That's what this book is about.

Dr. Dixon and I want to show you some ways in which you can enlist the help of your family in your efforts to stem overeating. We will give you scriptural guidelines for making positive changes in the way your family works so that you become a supportive, nurturing group. The benefits will go far beyond just overeating, and impact your family in a wonderful, constructive manner.

You don't have to be alone in your "thinning process." Your family may want to help you with a few changes prayerfully decided upon and carefully implemented.

Before we go on, you must understand that we are not taking the responsibility off you and putting it on the family. But you, while bearing the responsibility for what you eat, and what you weigh, can enlist the help of your family in helping you carry that responsibility better.

THINK ABOUT IT

Ask yourself the question: What would happen to my family if I were thin?

NOTES

1. Virginia Satir, *Conjoint Family Therapy* (Science and Behavior Books, 1982).

CHAPTER TWO

UNDERSTANDING THE CONNECTION

In this book we want to make you familiar with a term, "the family system."

It is a term that embraces both emotional and objective concepts. You will want a thorough understanding of the term so that you can begin to use it as a part of the communication processes within your family.

When we think of the word *family*, many pictures can come to mind. The elementary school workbooks, some years ago, gave us this image: a father going to work, wearing a suit or uniform; a mother staying home, wearing a dress and apron, usually caring for a child too young for school; an older brother carrying books and perhaps a mit and bat; and a sister, the middle child, pulling a wagon with puppies, kittens and/or dolls. Two parents, clearly defined roles and three happy, healthy, well-behaved children (who were also clean).

That family was not too much different from my own, except there were five children and the three oldest were girls (of which I am the youngest), and the two youngest were boys (and we weren't always clean).

That is a visual memory. I also have emotional concepts of what I think a family ought to be and provide: warmth, belonging, identity, a sense of "wantedness," safety, security, food, and fun. Sometimes, however, the emotional and visual memories are quite different from the ideal. Being right in the middle of a brood of five is a wonderful place sometimes and a terrible place at other times. My childhood memories of my family include both the wonderful and the terrible.

Likewise, many of you remember pain and rejection, poverty, fear, abuse, insecurity, ridicule, criticism, sexual molestation, drunken parents, yelling and neglect. So when mental images of the family arise, certain emotional connections are made as well. The result of peeling away our ideal images—a painful process—brings us to a truer understanding of the family system.

Therefore, Dr. Dixon and I add to a very emotionally charged image of the word *family* a cold and objective word—*system*, which means the logical and objective way something works.

Systems do what they do automatically. It is not a conscious mind-set or process, it is more mechanical. The purpose of my refrigerator, for example, is to keep my perishable food cold. The way it does that is by the system that is built into it.

When we combine the concepts of family and system into the concept "family system," we now have a logical and objective way to view how the family works. When I first started exploring this concept with Dr. Dixon, I had to come to understand that the system is not necessarily something that is set so solid that it cannot be changed.

As a little girl, I lived for a short while in McPherson, Kansas. To place a phone call I had to lift the receiver and wait for an operator to come on the line. She said "number please" and then connected me to whatever friend I wanted to speak with who also had a phone. But today it is quite different. The demands on the phone system due to the changing needs of the users no longer allow for the "number please" system. That way of doing things became outdated. I have stored away in a drawer a dial phone that works fine, but cannot handle the needs I have of using the new long distance services. A perfectly good system has been made useless by my changing needs.

It is the same in my family and in yours. My needs have changed, my children's needs have changed, my husband's needs have changed. Our needs have grown and swiftly become far too sophisticated for a "number please" type of family system.

Dr. Dixon and I have observed that a lack of success in dealing with overeating may in some cases lie in the fact that the family system needs to change to accommodate the change in behavior that you need to make. You see, when a demand is made on one part of the system to change (you, for example), demands are felt on the entire family system. When you make your needs known ("I can't handle pizza tonight"), it will affect the entire family system.

There is a definite connection between your family system—that is, the way your family handles problem situations—and your eating. In an effort to make this concept as clear as possible let me ask you these questions:

Do you find that you are the one making the sacrifices for the rest of the family? Will you eat barbequed pork ribs and potato salad with the family because it is their favorite instead of them eating broiled fish and baked potatoes with you?

Many overeaters have lost the ability to say, "I need you to sacrifice for me, to eat my food with me," and not feel guilty. A change in the way your family handles your overeating problem with you is appropriate. You can change, they can change. Your system can change.

"Hold everything right there!" you say. "If I asked my husband, right out of the blue, to change what he eats for me and my good, he would say, 'No way, this is stupid. I don't care what Neva Coyle or Dr. Dixon says, I am not going on a diet just so that you can lose weight. Leave me out of this. This is your problem.' "

Be patient, your family may not be ready to

handle this request. You see, just as a person has to mature, so do relationships. Your husband may be a mature, rational reasonable man and you may be, too. But has your relationship matured enough to handle requests such as I suggest?

It is possible that your family is not ready for this, yet. But with patience and prayer and working together that kind of loving maturity can come. For now, it is only important that you learn about the connections between your overeating habits and your family. In further chapters we will help you to see that we are not blaming the family for your overeating, but helping you to see their involvement. Our goal is for your family to become a part of your support system. We'll go into that in more detail as we go along.

THINK ABOUT IT

Are your emotional and visual memories of your childhood family different from your concept of the "ideal" family?

Are your emotional and visual memories of your *present* family different from your concept of the "ideal" family?

Has your family system changed to meet your changing needs?

Could your answers to any of the above questions have an impact on your eating and/or your weight?

CHAPTER THREE

RECONNECTING

In further chapters we will be dealing with the following issues: understanding the role of the family in your overeating; understanding that the family experiences of your past affect your family today; the support you can get from your family; what might be preventing their support; and how to make encouraging changes within yourself that your family will welcome.

But for now important groundwork must be laid. All that I have told you about the family system has its foundation in Scripture.

Some in our society have questioned the need for family. They say the family is "obsolete." Others, who still believe in the family, think that the maturing process between childhood and adulthood is the development from dependence to independence. But God did not design us to be independent, nor did He intend that we be dependent beyond childhood. With maturity we recognize our need for each other, and grow into healthy *inter*dependence. That, I believe, is the plan God has in mind.

The Lord doesn't expect any of us to be loners. It is His idea that we live, work and worship together and that we encourage one another. He designed us in such a way that we really do need each other.

We know, if we are familiar with 1 Corinthians 12, that every person who is a child of God, reborn by confessing faith in Jesus Christ as the Son of God, is not alone—that our problems, struggles and burdens are to be borne with the help of our brothers and sisters in Christ.

We also have been placed by God's design in a family. And in Genesis we have the basis for our first biblical description of what we know as the family.

Genesis 2:18:

The Lord God said, "It is not good for the man to be alone. I will make a helper suitable for him."

Here, our Creator indicates that His design and plan was for man to fully realize his humanity through companionship and reproductive partnership with his wife.

Again, in Genesis 2:24, we read:

For this reason a man will leave his father and mother and be united to his wife, and they will become one flesh.

This verse shows us that instead of remaining with his parents, under their protective custody, a man leaves them and, with his wife, establishes a new family unit.

The book of Ecclesiastes provides a graphic expression about that interdependency that is meant by the Lord for our lives.

Ecclesiastes 4:9–12 reads:

> Two are better than one, because they have
>   a good return for their work:
> If one falls down,
>   his friend can help him up.
> But pity the man who falls
>   and has no one to help him up!
> Also, if two lie down together, they will
>   keep warm.
> But how can one keep warm alone?
> Though one may be overpowered,
>   two can defend themselves.
> A cord of three strands is not quickly
>   broken.

On the basis of these scriptures, certain pictures come to mind.

We think, for example, of working at a job. There are things we do by ourselves that really stretch us. Sometimes, however, we get to the point where it is impossible to do any more alone. The encouragement of working together with another, the inspiration of sharing the task, the added energy, the strength that is shared by two may make the difference between the job getting done or not getting done. You multiply your efforts by working together. This is what is meant by "a good return for their labor."

Verse ten is especially touching. It says, "If one falls down, his friend can help him up." It is important to have a companion. Someone who can look out for you. If one falls, there is another who can help, who can lift up.

Identify the struggles in your life right now. There are so many ways to fall. The hurt and pain that comes from falling emotionally and spiritually is so much greater and longer lasting than the injury sustained in a physical fall.[1]

In his book *Stretcher Bearers*, Michael Slater says this about the story in Mark 2 about the four men carrying their friend to Jesus on a stretcher:

> The paralytic man truly needed his wonderfully determined friends to carry him and his problem to the feet of Jesus. If we understand this concept, then the miracle that took place in Mark 2 can take place in your life, in my life, and in the lives of many of our friends.[2]

Think of people who are just launching out into the adventure of serving God and moving ahead with His will for their lives. It's possible to fall while trying to do a good thing. When you are by yourself, the discouragement can be overwhelming. But in God's plan, it is meant that we would never be alone. He wants other human beings to be there—other believers who will share with us the adventure of moving ahead with His will in our lives. If one falls, the other can help in any way needed.

There is an interdependence here that is expressed so beautifully. No one likes to fall. But when you do it is special to have someone there to pick you up, to care for you, to encourage you—and you move on together. You need to release yourself from the tyranny of thinking that you will never fall. But *when* you fall, say to yourself: "I am not designed to make it alone. I need others. When I fall . . . I need others."

Reuben Welch, in his lovely book *We Really Do Need Each Other*, writes:

> The life that Jesus brings
>   is a shared life.
> The life of God in the world
>   does not have its meaning in isolated units,
>   but in a fellowship of those
>   who share that life in Him.[3]

The passage in Ecclesiastes says we need each other to keep warm. There is something so important and vital about the warmth of Christian fellowship. I need to have others around me who know me by name, love me and care for me. To be lonely is an awfully cold way to live.

> You see we really do need each other,
> not because of the inadequacies of God
> but because this is the way His grace works.[4]

That is the way He designed us.

In the *New Testament* we find more evidence that living in interdependence is God's will for our lives.

If you have any encouragement from being united with Christ, if any comfort from his love, if any fellowship with the Spirit, if any tenderness and compassion, then make my joy complete by being like-minded, having the same love, being one in spirit and purpose. Do nothing out of selfish ambition or vain conceit, but in humility consider others better than yourselves. Each of you should look not only to your own interests, but also to the interests of others. (Phil. 2:1–4)

Human beings develop through a series of social relationships and experiences. The family is that primary source of social relationships. Peer and work groups are other ways in which we develop socially and discover who we are. Meeting in small groups with fellow believers helps us develop spiritually. This type of meeting was the primary way the early church had of growing together.

When we put the concept of the family together with the healthy concept of interdependence, we now have a deeper understanding of what dynamic potential the Christian family has.

Christian families are to have intense care and deep sympathy for each other. All these benefits—encouragement, comfort, fellowship, tenderness and compassion—are viewed by Paul as present realities for us today.

Says Slater,

There is simply no way for people to make it socially, spiritually, and psychologically if they choose to go through life setting themselves apart from others. We all need other people. We need people in our lives who can touch in ways that are positive.[5]

Handling my problems alone can make me self-centered. But when I reach out to others—even for help—it works to release me from myself, better equipping me to contribute to the others in my family who, in return, might need my encouragement and support.

Because the family is designed by God to function as a unit, we can look at 1 Corinthians 12 with the family in mind and apply the principles we find there to the subject we are discussing here. Paul says:

> The body is a unit, though it is made up of many parts; and though all its parts are many, they form one body. (Verse 12)

Listen now to these instructions from God's Word:

> There should be no division. . . . Its parts should have equal concern over each other. (verse 25)

Also,

> If one part suffers, every part suffers with it; if one part is honored, every part rejoices with it. (Verse 26)

These principles, when placed within the context of family relationships, make us understand the scriptural significance of being supportive of each other through our efforts to break bad habits and the commitment to change our lifestyle. This has special meaning for the over-eater.

When I ask my family to sacrifice for me—to eat the food I need to eat and not eat the food that would tempt me—it brings them into an understanding of what it is like for me. It doesn't put the *focus* on me but on the problem they are helping me work through and solve. It enhances the "us" of our relationship.

Let us commit ourselves to make the determined effort to help our families meet such needs. Let our Christian families recognize and practice the concept of Christian interdependence.

THINK ABOUT IT

Do you feel alone in this battle?

Can you admit it when you fall?

Can you admit it to your family and ask for their help?

Would the practice of Christian interdependence in your own family help you deal with overeating?

NOTES

1. Special thanks to Pastor Ed Tedeschi of St. Paul, Minn., for a greater understanding of this biblical concept.
2. Michael Slater, *Stretcher Bearers* (Regal Books, 1985).
3. Reuben Welch, *We Really Do Need Each Other* (Grand Rapids, Mich.; Zondervan Publishing House, 1982).
4. Ibid.
5. Michael Slater, op. cit.

Chapter Four

DISCONNECTIONS

When you look at your own family with the understanding of Christian interdependence, you might be saying, "Yes, that is a perfect description of my family." But if you are among the average, even the norm for today's families, you are probably saying, "That is far from what my family is like."

The concept of Christian interdependence is an ideal for the family. But families, in reality, are far from the ideal.

This chapter, a little detour, is designed to help those with a painful past concerning their families. The biblical concepts set out here may be very basic for some, but for others I expect it will be the most important chapter of the whole book.

For many people, the word *family* can bring painful memories of physical, mental, sexual and/ or verbal abuse. Maybe you were in a family in which children were never heard, or had non-communicative parents who never shared themselves with you. In such families individuals polarize and become isolated. The family becomes "disjointed."

God's ideal for marriage, found in Genesis chapter one, is a picture of "jointedness." The Bible says, "Therefore shall a man leave [separate from] his father and his mother and shall cleave [be joined] unto his wife" (Gen. 2:24, KJV). But many times the "leaving and cleaving" concept is interrupted by interfering relatives, quarreling and competitive mates, or severed by the tragedy of divorce.

Recalling the pain inflicted on you by others in the family, or by remembering the pain you caused others, is truly unpleasant. Many people remember dishonesty and deceit in their families; friction, tension, coldness between feuding factions; fighting, jealousy and yelling between parents or siblings; drunkenness and beatings. All these things lead to a measure of insecurity and confusion.

"Neva," you say, "while painful for me to think about, this is an accurate picture of what my childhood family was like." If we were walking together right now, I would probably put my arm through yours in an effort to communicate my understanding and concern. "But," you might continue, "that was then, this is now. I am married and have children of my own. Do my childhood family experiences have an effect on us now?"

Yes, most definitely. Though you have left your parents in a tangible, physical sense, you may not have been able to leave them emotionally and I want you to see that for many there is definitely a connection between their past family experiences and their overeating behaviors. In a later chapter we'll talk more about how to make the healthy break with an unhealthy past.

You see, if the primary family system you were in as a child taught you deceit or perhaps "peace at any price," you have most likely brought those practices into your marriage and family. What's more, you are probably handing them on down to your children, along with the learned behavior your spouse brought into the marriage. Think of it as an emotional trousseau.

But I believe we can do something positive about it. I am firmly convinced that while we can't change the past, we can, with God's help, change the way the past affects us in the present. And that also changes the course of our future.

My mother said to me many times, during the season of adolescent heartbreaks, "Just think of this (whatever the painful event was) as another rung of the ladder of experience. Take the step up and grow from it." I would dry my tears, straighten my shoulders, hold up my chin and go on.

Her advice worked in those situations, but is this concept too simple when you are dealing with neglect, rape, or incest? I think that with God's loving, merciful touch of healing, you too can apply my mother's simple advice to the deep hurts and disappointments of your past.

What has this to do with overeating? Something very important. Many people eat to salve and bandage those old emotional cuts and bruises. But when God is allowed to heal those painful memories, the need for the overeating begins to go away. Then we can start to make lasting changes in old, overeating patterns.

The Bible says, in Ex. 15:26, "I am the Lord, who heals you." And again, in Ps. 147:3, "He heals the brokenhearted." Like magic? No, more like a miraculous work of mercy and love—slowly in some cases, more quickly in others, depending perhaps on the depth of the pain and how long you have carried it. But remember the promise of Phil. 1:6: "Being confident of this, that he who began a good work in you will carry it on to completion."

Maybe you *have* been disappointed and hurt in many ways by your earthly parents. But you can trust God the Father. How do I know? The Bible and experience tell me what God is like.

For some, "father" meant a workaholic and "mother," too busy to listen. But take heart in the comfort of Ps. 27:10: "Though my father and mother forsake me, the Lord will receive me."

Maybe your parents criticized and berated you—set you up for all kinds of emotional abuse. But God doesn't set you up; He sets you free. Many have been controlled and manipulated by families. But God wants only to guide and direct you on straight, safe paths.

Perhaps you were raised in such an atmosphere of perfection that you never quite "measured up." The Bible says we are in process, "being perfected":

> Not that I have already obtained all this, or have already been made perfect, but I press on to take hold of that for which Christ Jesus took hold of me. (Phil. 3:12)

In 2 Cor. 13:11, Paul says: "Aim for perfection." That gives us a goal to be reaching for, giving meaning to our struggles and efforts.

Others have had all their decisions made for them. But our loving God wants you to see the choices *you* can make, on your own. His wisdom is available to help you avoid mistakes.

> Surely you desire truth in the inner parts; you teach me wisdom in the inmost place. (Ps. 51:6)

> If any of you lacks wisdom, he should ask God, who gives generously to all without finding fault, and it will be given to him. (James 1:5)

His love and mercy also is available to you to help you overcome mistakes you have already made.

> His mercy extends to those who fear him, from generation to generation. (Luke 1:50)

> But because of his great love for us, God, who is rich in mercy, made us alive with Christ even when we were dead in transgressions—

it is by grace you have been saved. (Eph. 2: 4–5)

Some have been beaten and raped by their dads. I assure you, God will not violate you. He will hold you, but not crush you. He will love you, freely, without price on your part.

But you are a shield around me, O Lord, My Glorious One, who lifts up my head. (Ps. 3:3)

O house of Israel, trust in the Lord—he is their help and shield. (Ps. 115:9)

The name of the Lord is a strong tower; the righteous run to it and are safe. (Prov. 18:10)

God is aware of the sins and even crimes committed against you and He did something about it. He sent His Son Jesus to die for all those sins.

For God so loved [put your name here] that he gave his one and only son, that whoever believes in him [do you believe in him?] shall not perish but have eternal life. (John 3:16)

Every pain that you have experienced at the hands of your family, Jesus took to the cross with Him. You don't have to bear it anymore. He has borne it for you.

"But, Neva," you say, through tears of pain-ful memories, "you weren't there. It was as though God forgot me. He protected everyone else, but He forgot me." You are not the only one who has ever felt this way and thought that God had overlooked his pain.

> But Zion said, "The Lord has forsaken me, the Lord has forgotten me."

> [To which the Lord replied:] "Can a mother forget the baby at her breast and have no compassion for the child she has borne? Though she may forget, I will not forget you! See, I have engraved you on the palms of my hands; your walls are ever before me." (Isa. 49:14–16)

Those engravings, my friend, are in the form of horrendous nail scars. Whenever Jesus looks at those scars, He sees you and me.

God has never forsaken or abandoned us. And if you are ever going to fully realize the support and help that can be yours through your family system, you must be healed from the pain of your past by allowing Him to handle those hurtful memories. You must be able to separate from the old system in order to work on and modify the present system, and the way it influences your overeating.

For example: There once was a time in which I was afraid to trust anyone. I had been hurt and even betrayed by a few people whom I had trusted as friends. I had successfully completed building a thick and secure wall around my emotions, and every new relationship was kept safely outside that wall. One day a person trying to get close to me approached me in tears and said, "Don't make me pay for the wrong things that others have done to you."

That was an important lesson for me to learn. My friend's advice was sound, and I made the decision to let every relationship that I am in stand on its own merit.

Do you make your present family pay for the wrong things your former family did to you? Do you mistrust your spouse? Based on what—the wrong things they have actually done or the wrong things you saw your father do to your mother? Is your present husband suspect because of what your ex-husband did to you?

One woman told me that when her husband was a few minutes late coming home, she was stricken with panic. Sometimes she would be hard on herself for experiencing such emotions. But if her husband was more than a few minutes late, or if she did not approve of what he was doing when they were apart, she would find her panic turning to anger and distrust. Not so incidentally, she overate during such times.

Finally, she realized that her husband had not really done anything to merit such intense feelings of mistrust and anger. As she committed this area of her life to God, she realized that it was her ex-husband's behavior that had conditioned her for such reactions. She had to reach into the painful past and find release through forgiveness. Then she was able to gain insight into her problem. When she did this, she noticed that her eating habits also changed.

Do you have negative emotions toward your

teenaged children because of the way your adolescent brothers and sisters treated you when you were living together as a family many years ago? Or do you mistrust your children because you were not trustworthy as a youngster?

I know a young girl whose father suddenly became insanely jealous when she reached puberty. As she reached dating age, he accused her of sleeping with every boyfriend. When she denied it, he accused her of lying and told her she was a tramp. When she experimented with new hairstyles and makeup, he went into tirades, saying she just did this to get every boy she could to notice her.

Many times the young girl cried and begged her father to stop saying such things. He slapped her and told her that to call her father a liar was disrespectful. He dished out punishment that far exceeded her "crimes."

Only after she became a grown woman did she realize what had happened to her as she heard her father and his brothers reminisce about the terrible things they did in their adolescence. She heard them bragging about their sexual adventures and experimentation. Then she understood that the cruel things her father did to her were because of what *he* had done when he was growing up.

Up until then, she had always feared her father, and had an unbearable sense of failure. However, when she realized the truth, she then began to hate him. Unable to express her painful feelings, she overate, which gave her feelings of power, control and comfort. The weight she gained as a result also gave her protection from relationships with men, who she felt were dirty and lustful.

Such past experiences can leave us all with a sense of unfinished business long after our parents are gone. It is also recognized that even our concept of God is directly related to the relationship we had with our earthly fathers. If that relationship was or still is a painful one, your relationship with God can be affected in many ways.

How about you? Do you have any unfinished business in regard to your childhood family? If so, it must be taken care of before you can make progress toward the ideal that God has for your family system.

My point is this: What good is a diet book if you can't stick with it? There are some issues that cannot be resolved simply by keeping perfect calorie sheets. Sometimes there are painful emotions from the past that are behind eating patterns. This book does not replace those helpful and essential diet and nutritional publications, but approaches an entire area those books do not even begin to touch.

Most of us understand the connection between calories and dieting, but do we understand the connection between eating and the emotions? Do we understand the connection between the emotions and the family? You see, when we can picture those connections, then we are able to make the first step toward becoming free—and gaining control of our eating habits.

THINK ABOUT IT

Do you have emotionally painful memories?

Do you eat to salve emotional pain?

Could there be a connection between a painful past and your present overeating and/or weight problem?

CHAPTER FIVE

EATING AND EMOTIONS

In this chapter I'm not going to address weight loss, per se, but rather consider the concept that overeating is an alternative approach to emotional pain.

In an article from the *Journal of the American Medical Association*, January 1970, we find the following:

> Clearly, achievement of weight loss should not be utilized as the end point of therapy, but rather treatment of the basic underlying emotional problems must be incorporated into the program.

Being overweight has much pain associated with it. Sometimes the pain is a result of being overweight; other times the overweight is the result of pain.

Overeaters have a common complaint that they are not understood or that their problems are really more special than the problems of others. These false accusations against the rest of the world have to be confronted and overcome. Otherwise they will prevent help coming from thin pastors, counselors and doctors. If the overeater can get past the "nobody understands me" syndrome and realize that even the thinnest person still has emotional pain, then he is on his way to a solution.

The emotional pain experienced by the overweight person is sometimes like being on a cruel merry-go-round. At this point in your life, you may be hurting because you are fat. Let's say that you deal with emotional pain by eating. You know that eating only compounds the problem, but you don't know how to break the cycle. In order to put this area of your life right, you must understand where the problem began.

I would suggest that you may be carrying around things from your first family, your childhood, that you have really outgrown and need to discard. One of those things is the way you handle events in your life that cause you emotional pain. David Seamands, in *Putting Away Childish Things*, says, "Any experience for which you do not make the required payment of emotion, you will later pay for with compounded interest."[1]

It was in your family or the setting in which you were raised that you learned to handle pain. The way you dealt with your emotions was part of your childhood training. Your temperament also has a part in how you deal with emotions, but the process of handling those emotions in acceptable ways is taught within the family.

This one thing I know for sure: fat or thin, short or tall, male or female, many people are using food and its temporary comfort, enjoyment, pleasure (even the chemical "high" that certain foods provide), instead of dealing with emotionally painful situations and events.

Do you? Would you like to find out for sure? Then let me ask you some questions.

Do you handle any of the following feelings by eating?

_____ Insecurity

_____ Jealousy

_____ Rejection

_____ Worry

_____ Stress

_____ Anger

_____ Grief

_____ Fear

_____ Sadness

_____ Depression

_____ Joy

_____ Guilt.

Now ask yourself these questions: Do I reach for food for comfort? Do I eat when I am not hungry for food, but for love? Acceptance? Affection? Recognition? Did you answer yes to any of these?

Does my present family give me the support I need when I have to handle painful emotions? Do I get comfort when I need it from my family? Does my family give me the expressions of love that I need? Did you answer no to any of these?

Facing some of these issues can be painful. But keep reading! *Whatever you do, don't run away and eat.* You'll be glad you stuck around and faced this. You will grow and so will your family.

I know that I have given you something to think about. You may want to come back to this section again and think it through after you have read the entire chapter. But let me continue to direct you into a deeper understanding.

Think with me about a little baby, not quite an infant, not quite a toddler. The mother playfully asks, "Where's your nose?" Baby smiles and with his little, pudgy hand full of graham cracker crumbs finds his nose. Mother laughs out loud and praises him.

Now Mother tries to trick him. "Where are your *toes*?" Baby lifts both feet effortlessly and grabs his toes. Mom tickles and kisses him while they both laugh.

She is teaching him, through this game, to know the parts of his body. This is vital to a child's body awareness.

I had taught my children, just like the mother in our example, how to touch and identify their noses, and toes, tummies, ears and eyes. However, I remember when my children were babies, and one of them came to me holding her stomach. She said, "I have a headache in my tummy." She made an accurate assumption of the symptoms, but an incorrect diagnosis.

One area where many families fail is in teaching little ones what is happening when they get in touch with their feelings, and how to handle those feelings.

It is in our family upbringing that the "accepted" ways of expressing feelings and emotions are defined. These accepted ways, however, are not necessarily the best and most healthy for us, but were the most *comfortable* ways for the family.

The family, then, is where the primary emotional needs are supposed to be met. That is where we learn either to rightly handle our pain or to deny it; to approach emotionally difficult situations or to avoid them; we learn to cope emotionally or to become destructive.

One of our first needs is a place to belong—to know that we are of value and that no one can take our place. Whether or not the family system you entered as a baby could handle that need and fill it sufficiently affects the way you see yourself; or in other words, it helped to form your self-image.

A basic principle for understanding the definition of the family system was stated in a previous chapter: "The family's established method or procedure of doing something."

Now connect that to our emotional needs.

Then the statement reads: "The family's established method or procedure of handling emotionally painful events."

Sometimes the family's "established method" is to delay, deny, replace, or avoid painful emotions. That is the beginning of trouble.

Emotions and feelings are part of what makes us human. And when those feelings and emotions are stifled, we become less than what God designed us to be. When we lose touch with our feelings, we are of less use to those in need of our understanding and compassion.

In *The Curate's Awakening* by George MacDonald, I came across a passage that made me think about these concepts:

> Sometimes a thunderbolt will shoot from a clear sky; and sometimes in the life of a peaceful individual, without warning of gathered storm, something terrible will fall.[2]

This, to me, is a perfect description of one of life's many crises. Many times, a crisis comes suddenly, but just as often, it comes with the "warning of gathered storm" that has been ignored by those around the individual. MacDonald goes on:

> And from that moment [of crisis] everything is changed. That life is no more what it was. Better it ought to be, worse it may be. The result depends on the life itself and its response to the invading storm of trouble.[3]

Our responses are encouraged or taught,

whether overtly or covertly, by our early experiences in our family. We learned early what was the acceptable way to handle our "thunderbolt" experiences—whether or not it was safe to express our feelings. If our family was open to tears, we could cry. If not, we learned to stifle those childhood sobs—and along with them our pain. Often, we interpreted that to also mean, "Don't let your hurt or discomfort show. Do something else with your pain besides involving the people around you."

For many of us, it meant *eat*.

Let me ask you a few more questions: Can you associate any type of trauma with the onset of your weight problem? Think about it. For instance, do you handle emergencies well? How is your eating then? What about several hours later? Or even days later?

Your family system is where you learned to deal with emergencies and the emotionally painful issues of life. When you realize those two statements are true, you may want to make some necessary breaks from the family system of the past, and some changes in your present family system as well.

You see, an eating disorder[4] is one of the ways in which people learn to avoid, delay, deny or replace emotional pain. But an eating disorder is only one of the many means of dealing with emotional pain or emotionally painful events.

Others may overwork or overinvolve themselves in hobbies or causes. Dad may work obsessively on his car, while Mom may be overcommitted in clubs, classes and organizations. There are myriad alternatives that people can come up with to avoid dealing directly with pain. Eating is only one of those alternatives.

Let's look at some illustrations.

June can't face the disappointments in her life at the moment. Her marriage, her job, her church and the fact that she was not elected chairman of a committee she is serving on are all painful to her. She is overeating to deal with the pain instead of confronting the issues.

But June has learned a "secret" way to control her weight. She uses bulemic behaviors—what we know as the binge/purge syndrome. She throws up after overeating, usually huge amounts of food after one indulgence.

Even though much information is now available on bulemic practices and has helped many stem this destructive behavior, it has also served to instruct and encourage others to begin these dangerous practices to control their weight while continuing to overeat. It has become more acceptable to become bulemic than to be overweight.

The trademark of the bulemic is the need to be in control. Many times as children, these women have heard over and over again, "For heaven's sake, control yourself." And when they have practiced long enough, they learn how to control almost everything and everyone around them in an effect to hide the fact that they really can't control themselves.

Meg cannot face her disappointments either, but can't or won't throw up when she overeats. She gets fat. But being fat is still another disappointment, which requires more overeating to make her feel better about that. She might even select close friends who are fat—preferably fatter than herself—who will help justify and reinforce her overeating and obesity.

Is disappointment the only reason for overeating?

There are some people who would rather sit in front of the TV with a bag of Doritos and a six-pack of beer than to confront a husband or wife with problems in the relationship.

There are those who wolf down donuts and cookies by the dozen because they are lonely and in need of love.

Some reach for Twinkies, instead of praying and trusting God for a financial need.

Many mistakenly assume overeating solves the problem. But the most disappointing thing of all is that food doesn't take away the problem and in many cases only makes it all worse.

It would be far better to confront the issue head-on than to overeat when you feel neglected or angry. Sidney Simon says, in *Negative Criticism*,

> Look for what it is that you really want to tell the other person. It would be far better to say, "Hey, please, I love you. I want you to

pay more attention to me, show me that you care, share more of yourself with me. I love you and need you. I can't do without you."[5]

You don't have to avoid confronting your problems. You don't have to turn to overeating as a more comfortable means of handling your painful feelings. You know that overeating ends up being more troublesome than if the feelings had been confronted initially. Problems are not solved through alternative processes, but through confrontation.

You can change the destructive overeating patterns in your life by letting God do a work in your emotions and the ways in which you have been taught to deal with your feelings.

Let me offer a word of advice. You may not be able to get in touch with your most painful feelings all by yourself. You may need help. Many people do. It is not a disgrace or to your shame that you are out of touch with some deep personal feelings. If you sense that this is an area in which you could use a little help, please make an appointment with your pastor. Ask him to help you or to refer you to someone qualified to help you.

I like what David Seamands says:

Feelings are important, and there is a central place in the Christian religion for the emotional life. The fruit of the Spirit is love, joy, peace, and all three of these include feelings. Christianity is not a form of stoicism. It in no way relegates the emotions to a second-class status, but recognizes that wholeness must include the emotional life. One of the characteristics of life in the Holy Spirit is the free flow of all that is deepest in the human personality. The Spirit frees us to experience and express our emotions.[6]

Your family may have taught you to deal with emotions inappropriately. But the Holy Spirit can reach deep within you and "undo" and "redo" and set you free emotionally. It is the work of the mercy and grace of God that can make you whole and strong enough to disconnect from the family system of the past and be reconnected with your emotions in a healthy way. You can confront emotionally painful issues and events without overeating.

THINK ABOUT IT

Do you eat when you have nothing to do?

Do you eat when you are bored and restless? Anxious, worried or tense? Depressed or discouraged? Feeling lonely? Under stress? Excited?

Are you willing to let the Holy Spirit heal your emotions so that you do not have to eat in these situations? Let us move on now to examine how this is done.

NOTES

1. David Seamands, *Putting Away Childish Things* (Victor Books, 1982).
2. George MacDonald, *The Curate's Awakening* (Minneapolis: Bethany House Publishers, 1985).
3. Ibid., op. cit.
4. The American Psychiatric Association lists in their *Diagnostic and Statistical Manual of Mental Disorders* (DSM III) anorexia and bulimia as eating disorders. Overeating is not treated as an eating disorder if it results in being overweight. However, Dr. Dixon and I agree that overeating of any kind for any emotional need and/or pain is an eating disorder.
5. Sidney Simon, *Negative Criticism* (Argus, 1978).
6. David Seamands, op. cit.

CHAPTER SIX

PUTTING THE PAST IN THE PAST

A man will leave his father and mother and be united to his wife, and they will become one flesh" (Genesis 2:24). In an earlier chapter we explored this verse as it relates to forming a new family system. Now let's talk a bit more about the "leaving" concept. In order to make a break with the destructive patterns taught in the old family system, you will need to understand how that system worked—and how God can work through it in you.

Perhaps the most common type of pain from our past comes from the hurtful words spoken by those we loved and trusted.

Some have heard:

"I don't like you."

"I don't love you anymore."

"You are too fat."

"You are ugly."

"You don't deserve anything better."

"You don't do anything right."

"Can't you ever learn anything?"

Maybe you have heard these actual words, or have interpreted behaviors and insinuations, investing them with the same meanings.

Words can't be taken back. They either build or bruise. Harsh, destructive words spoken in the context of the most dependent relationship of all, that of parent-child, can absolutely destroy.

Unfortunately, the negative words you heard as a child from your parents were more readily received than the positive ones. When negative words and actions are repeated, they begin to strike the familiar thought carried within since the last time they were spoken. Those negative expressions begin to form and then confirm hidden fears. Negative words sometimes have to be spoken only once for the damage to be done, while positive words may have to be repeated again and again—and even then they are not often believed.

I think most parents are quicker to use negative words than positive words in dealing with their children, maybe because children usually do more things that require correction than affirmation. Parents seldom recognize that they can affirm a child just for *being*, not doing.

Sometimes just the lack of affirmation from those closest and most important can lead to chronic discouragement. As adults we can look in the Bible and find good examples of dealing with discouragement. For the most part we can find comfort from the Psalms, or instruction from the Proverbs. But children do not know how to "find" encouragement.

How about you? Do you remember discouragement and negativity in your childhood? Did you finally accept discouragement as a part of life? Could you be carrying that practice over into your own family? Most likely, you didn't have the resources then to lift the discouragement from your life, or how to react in a mature fashion to the negativity heaped on you. But it's not too late! You can learn how to deal with and be healed from the pain you have carried all these years.

The emotional pain and discouragement you are experiencing, no matter what the source, can cause you, if you take the opportunity, to become an overcomer. You can be free from the past, and you can grow from it. And the first step is to make the attempt toward understanding not only the pain from the past but the people of your past as well.

Let's talk about Mother for a moment. Was she perfect? Mothers get impatient, tired, stretched and stressed just like the rest of the general population. Mothers are people, too. Sidney Simon says, in *Negative Criticism*:

> It is very difficult to find a mother who feels she is really doing her job well. And for the record, most fathers feel even worse about their overall performance.[1]

Perhaps as we get older we understand more what mothers are like and what makes a good mother. (It's too bad that we don't know this when we start out raising children instead of after the work is done.) Even though Mother has the most influence on the children early in their lives, emotional pain can be inflicted by other important family members as well. Many have been hurt deeply by their fathers.

In the research that Dr. Dixon and I undertook for this book, many told us of incidents of incest, rape, verbal and physical abuse in their families. Others told us of sexual molestation from outside the family which they could not share with their parents. Because of closed family systems, they have carried this devastating emotional pain into the present. The fact that the people in our study are overeaters holds special significance. Wounds that happen within the family system will often result in people trying to compensate for the pain through overeating.

When the abused person leaves the family (usually, as soon as he can through early marriage or by taking a job and moving out), he still has the unfinished business of his emotional pain. Instead of finding that physical separation from the family is freeing, often he is held even emotionally tighter to the family through guilt. Then, instead of breaking the patterns of the old family system, they are repeated in new relationships formed.

Think about your relationship to your parents. As a child, those were your most vital relationships. When you think of your childhood home and family, remember that even then families were under attack. The pressures of making a living, disciplining the children, the lack of preparation for parenting, as well as adulterous parents, alcoholism, materialism, and the changing society all brought attacks upon the family and its members. Today, those pressures are magnified tremendously.

In *Signs of the Times*, May 1984, we find an article on children of alcoholics:

> There are twelve to fifteen million children under eighteen living in alcoholic homes today.

> Long before alcoholism is ever identified the children learn to deny, minimize, discount and rationalize, all of which distorts their perception of reality.

> We can certainly offer education to help to clarify for that child what it is that's going on. We can help him to feel less ashamed and less isolated and to see that he has other choices in his life. The first thing he needs to know is that he's not responsible for the unhappiness and the drinking in his home. But he does need to take the responsibility that he doesn't repeat the pattern.[2]

Maybe there wasn't alcoholism in your family, but you need to take the responsibility that you don't repeat whatever destructive patterns were present in your childhood family.

In 1986, the Christian Broadcasting Network released these statements under the heading, "Families on the Faultlines":

- Up to nine million people in the U.S. suffer from depression, most of them women.
- Sixty percent of second marriages also end in divorce.
- Father-deprivation can be directly tied to murder, rape and assault.
- Most single-parent homes are headed by women with severely emotionally scarred children.
- Divorced women and their children have an immediate 73 percent drop in living standard.

Think, for a moment, not of the children in these frightening statistics, but of the parents. They are people with a past. In trying to understand your childhood—to put the past in the past—try also to understand your parents as children. What kind of family system did they grow up in? Look at your parents, not through the eyes of your childhood self, but as an adult. Try to understand that only people with severe problems, people away from God's divine will and pattern for living, hurt their children to the degree that you may have been hurt. Try to separate yourself from the child in the scenes imbedded in your memory. Look at them with the eyes of an adult, who now has a broader perspective on the fallen condition of mankind.

Did you ever consider your most hurtful parent as having emotional problems? Did you ever think when they were yelling at you that the situation simply gave them an opportunity to yell and that you were just handy? That it really had nothing to do with you at all?

I'm not taking their side or defending them—only trying to give you some understanding that your parents were just as human and frail in their humanity as you are. They may have come from systems just as faulty as the one they passed on to you.

The "pained" inflict pain, carrying on destruction from generation to generation. If you don't want to pass this practice on to your children, now is the time to make this break and put the past in the past.

Let's take the tendency to criticize, which many parents pass on their children. Ask yourself these questions: When you were criticized, did you tend to overeat? Did you reach for food to comfort you?

Criticism is one thing that drives us to overeating. There are others.

I myself came from a family of nonconfronters. (I expect that if any of them read this book, they will deny it, as true nonconfronters would.) In our family system, we "confronted" the issues by talking to someone other than the person with whom we had the problem.

I also married a nonconfronter. We lived many years in nonconfrontive ways—and I ate.

Only in the last few years have we begun to learn how to be confrontive. I thought that being confrontive was opening myself and my marriage up to free-wheeling criticism and nagging, but it hasn't. Instead it has brought times of closeness and solution. Confrontation has forced growth. It has had a direct and positive effect on my eating. We made healthy breaks from our past. We decided to put into our system room for confrontation, which by the way, also gave us room for verbal affirmation, which was desperately needed.

"OK," you might be saying, "I see the need to disconnect from the family system that taught me destructive ways to handle situations. But how?"

Phil. 3:13, 14 records Paul's decision to make a healthy break with his past. He said, "Forgetting those things which are behind, and reaching forth unto those things which are before, I press toward the mark" (KJV).

Says Dan Betzer, in a December 1986 article in the *Pentecostal Evangel*:

No more counterproductive activity ever plagued humanity than resentment. I have known people who have gone to their graves holding deep grudges and resentments over unintentional wounds to the spirits and egos. What a waste! That's like throwing away a vault of gold bars because the price of the metal went down a few cents per ounce temporarily. It's like destroying a car because it's out of gas or needs a tune-up.[3]

"But," many of you are saying, "these wounds that were inflicted on my spirit were intentional."

I realize that. But intentional or unintentional, the solution is not found in holding on to the bitterness. Even if the offense does not deserve forgiveness, you will not be free until you forgive.

Will you stop allowing past resentments to steal moments from the present? Can you realize that the only sinless person who ever lived was Christ? Only when you can begin to forgive your parents and others for the painful memories of your past can you be freed from its damaging effects.

There comes a time for forgiving. That time is now. You will never be able to fully forget, but through forgiveness you can take the sting out of those remembrances. You may not know how, but are you at least *willing* for someone to show you how?

Forgiveness is a miraculous healer. You may not fully understand it, but forgiveness does not have to be understood to make it a workable principle. Only when you ask God to help you forgive those who have hurt you can you begin to disconnect from the faulty family system. And later, when you have gained some perspective through forgiveness, you will be able to see the good that can come from it.

In his book *Reality Therapy*, William Glasser says:

> Irresponsibility is never justified no matter how much one has suffered at the hands of others.[4]

Tough stuff? Not when you have the dynamic of Christ's love and forgiveness working through your life, reaching the pain and terrors of your past. Letting Christ touch your inmost secret pain and fear is a responsibility you hold. And His touch alone brings wholeness and sets you free to pursue your own life with a solid foundation.

Is there someone in your mind right now whom you need to forgive for pain inflicted on you in the past. A parent? A grandparent? Some other trusted adult? A sibling? Don't let another moment go by before you stop and ask God to help you forgive that offender. Ask God to take away the bitterness and unforgiveness from your own heart. Ask Him to forgive you for being hardened by unforgiveness. Lift up to God and give to Him those memories that haunt you. Tell Him of your desire to disengage your present behaviors from the negative influences of your past. Ask Him for help. He is there, listening, and will answer your prayer.

Not only can you be free from the pain of the past, you can let Christ work in you in such a way as to become better for it.

The Bible does not promise that you would

not experience the discomfort and suffering that comes from criticism, abuse or rejection. But it does tell us that, in that suffering, you will be able to find God in a special way. That is, of course, if you turn to Him for help.

In *Free to Grieve*, Maureen Rank says:

> The Bible has much to say about the good that can come from suffering. You'll be able to comfort others when you have suffered yourself. Suffering builds patience and god-liness and hope. Hurting refines your faith, so it will be strong and sure. A pain endured can lead to a special depth of friendship and identification with Christ. And much, much more.

> It's not that I'm glad for the suffering itself, but God has taken that suffering and, through it, produced so much good that I am glad for having gone through those losses. This deeper pain has somehow opened in me a deeper capacity for deeper joy.[5]

Can God actually take the past, *your* past, and use it for good? Yes, yes, He can! Can He actually take the suffering you have experienced and both rescue you and redeem the situation and use it for good? Yes—if you are willing to let Him help you through forgiveness, put the past in the past, and profit from the pain in such a way that you will have a stronger and more secure future trusting totally in Him.

Heb. 13:5–6 declares:

God has said,

"Never will I leave you;
  Never will I forsake you."
So we say with confidence,
  "The Lord is my helper;
    I will not be afraid.
  What can man do to me?"

Dr. Charles Stanley, author and pastor, says:

God wrapped Himself in human flesh and came into this world so that we might understand that He fully understands what is going on in our hearts and lives. . . .

What He came to do in all of our lives is to make us complete, whole, the total person that God wants us to be. The Bible says, 'No creature is hidden from His sight.' No one can suffer outside the reality and the realm of the presence of God. You can't even hurt privately. . . . There is nothing hidden from the eyes of Jesus. But they are not eyes of condemnation, of judgment, of curiosity, or criticism. They are the eyes of love. . . . Isn't that a comfort?

The love of God flows into your life, overwhelming you, driving out the sense of rejection, driving out that sense of inadequacy, driving out that sense of incompetence in your life, the inferiority, the ideas that you don't belong.[6]

Only the mercy and grace of God reaching into your life right where you are now can help you sort out all the hurts and heal them. He can help you sort out all the confusion and give you answers. As David says in Psalm 18:16–19:

> He reached down from on
>   high and took hold of me;
> He drew me out of deep
>   waters.
> He rescued me from my
>   powerful enemy,
> from my foes, who were
>   too strong for me.
> They confronted me in the
>   day of my disaster,
> but the Lord was my
>   support.
> He brought me out into a
>   spacious place;
> He rescued me because He
>   delighted in me.

Did you feel that you would never measure up when your mother criticized you? Forgive her and let it go. Let the fact that you feel so unworthy point you to God's grace and mercy in a way many people never experience.

Do you feel dirty and cheap because your father or brother molested or beat you? Instead of pursuing a destructive course, let the past motivate you toward understanding others who are experiencing indescribable pain.

Did you feel picked on when your grandfather teased you until you cried? Realize that you did not have a perfect, all-American grandpa. Then reach out in love and acceptance to someone who is feeling alone and rejected.

Do you feel abandoned and cheated because your mother gave you up for adoption? You may still want to find her for a sense of identity, but you won't have any chance of ever getting to know her if you are angry and if you do get to meet her at last. Let the pain and questions you have give you new understanding as you seek God on a deeper level. His entire "family" is built through adoption.

Do you feel inferior, dumb and worthless because of your interpretation of the actions and expressions of your parents? Find out who you are in Christ and grow and breathe deep in that knowledge. Then share your discovery with someone else who is hurting.

Did you feel your parents were too strict? Maybe they were driven by fear or some guilt from their past—who knows? You can stand fast in the liberty of Christ.

Through forgiveness you will be able to put it all behind and press on—to make the changes necessary in your present family system. Receive the precious gift from God; let Him heal you and work in you in such a wonderful way that it affects your family today.

"Let a man leave his parents . . . a woman as well . . . and cling to his wife." Leave the old system behind, through forgiveness, and determine in your own heart that your home will be a positive and supportive force in the lives of your family.

Listen to these marvelous words from Romans 8:28:

> And we know with an absolute knowledge that for those who are loving God, all things are working together resulting in good, for those who are called ones according to His purpose. (Wuest's *Word Studies*, Vol. 1)

Let a loving, caring God help you by teaching you forgiveness and working a miracle. You will find peace for the present and a positive attitude toward the future if the past is relegated safely to the realm of the yesterdays. The pain can be redeemed and used to bring healing and release to many others if you will only allow God to work in and through you.

Jude 1 and 2 says:

> To those who have been called, who are loved by God the Father and kept by Jesus Christ: mercy, peace and love be yours in abundance.

Are you ready to go on to look at some of the more specific ways in which your family can change in order to be more of a support to you in your "thinning process"? Are you ready to look at some of the ways in which you can change your behavior toward your family as well? With the foundation behind us and a broad understanding of the family and the important part it plays in each of our lives, we are now ready to take a closer look at some of the more specific issues involved.

THINK ABOUT IT

Can you see ways in which your childhood family was under attack?

Do you see how each of your parents was a "target"?

Are you willing to forgive those in your past who have hurt you?

NOTES

1. Sidney Simon, *Negative Criticism* (Argus, 1978).
2. *Signs of the Times* (May 1984).
3. Dan Betzer, *Pentecostal Evangel* (December 1986).
4. William Glasser, *Reality Therapy* (New York: Harper & Row Publishers, 1965).
5. Maureen Rank, *Free to Grieve* (Minneapolis: Bethany House Publishers, 1985).
6. Dr. Charles Stanley, *The Helper for the Hurting*, Audio tape.

CHAPTER SEVEN

FAMILY SABOTAGE

We have been talking about the past. Now let's look closely at the present. How does your present family system affect your dieting process?

Have you ever attempted to lose weight and felt that one or more members of your family was fighting your progress in some way? Does that sound like a silly question?

You might think so. But in our research, the response to that question was overwhelmingly in the affirmative.

Think about it again.

Think about your attempts to lose weight—what we call "the thinning process." Have you ever felt that your family was consciously and verbally supporting your efforts, but through their attitudes or behaviors sabotaging your progress?

When a family enters into any kind of change, its members either consciously or unconsciously enter a process of examining what the change will mean to them. For example, when you plan a vacation, you anticipate the cost and implement a savings program. Many times a budget overhaul is necessary. Perhaps it's the first time the family really takes a good look at their money and the way it's handled. Suddenly, every purchase has to meet certain criteria. It takes this kind of effort for the family to afford the vacation. It is the same when the family becomes a support system to help the overeater.

Sometimes the family will unknowingly sabotage your efforts to change your eating habits, ways of handling problems and emotions—all your efforts to get thin.

Let's begin with our definition of sabotage as it applies to overeating or the thinning process.

Family sabotage is: The behavior of one family member that discourages and/or undermines the efforts toward change in another.

Recently, I was teaching a "Free To Be Thin" class at my church and decided to invite all the spouses of overeaters as well. It was an interesting group. Some spouses came, even though they didn't see the need. Others encouraged their spouse to *skip* the class that night and attend a banquet the church was having! Still others just refused to come and some of the class members stayed home. There were a few that came alone, but most of the twenty-five people who came were with their husbands or wives. I taught a simple overview of the family system and went into detail about sabotage versus support and how the spouse can help or hinder. I got an interesting response within the next few days.

One woman called me and said, "We started fighting on the way home. It lasted for another whole evening when my husband got home from work.

"My husband doesn't see how his eating relates at all to my diet."

"Does it?" I asked.

"Of course it does!" she replied angrily.

"How?" I pressed.

"When he eats my favorite things in front of me, it tempts me. Then he actually *offers* them to me. I can't resist, and he knows it!"

"Does that sabotage your diet?"

"Yes," she sobbed.

"Does your husband sabotage your diet?"

"He doesn't mean to—" I could tell she was confused.

"But does he?"

"*He* doesn't see it that way."

"Listen to the question. Does it sabotage your diet when your husband eats food in front of you that you want to avoid in order to lose weight?"

"Yes."

"Does your husband sabotage your diet when he does this?"

A pause. Then a quiet response, "Yes, but. . . ."

The confusion comes in understanding the difference between conscious and unconscious sabotage. The dictionary uses words like "intentional" and "deliberate" when defining sabotage. Most of us do not want to admit that our spouse would intentionally and deliberately undermine our thinning process. Let's look at Webster's definition without using the words "intentional" and "deliberate":

> sab-o-tage—obstruction of, or damage to any cause, movement, activity, effort, etc.

We can accept that definition. But when we add the word "deliberate," we become very uncomfortable. We need to understand that, while it may be intentional, it is most likely unconscious. A deliberate act of sabotage has the same effect whether it is conscious or not.

Listen to this conversation between husband and wife on the phone late one afternoon.

"Hello, sweetheart. Would you like to go out for pizza tonight?"

"But, darling, you know I'm trying to lose weight and I don't think I could handle pizza tonight."

"Oh, c'mon, I really wanted to take you out for pizza."

"Hey, don't you want me to get thin?"

"Sure I do. But I also want to eat pizza tonight and I want you to go with me."

"Listen to me, dear," she says. "I have been

struggling all day with temptations. First it was the doughnuts you brought home for breakfast. Then when I was out with the girls for lunch, they all wanted to order dessert. I wouldn't eat dessert and they called me a party-pooper. Now it's suppertime and I was planning to fix a salad and some broiled trout. Wouldn't that be o.k.?"

"Think of a pizza. Thick crust, pepperoni, olives, onions and lots of cheese. Doesn't that sound better?"

"I thought you liked trout."

"I do. But tonight I want pizza."

"I can't handle it. You go without me."

"I don't want to go without you. If your diet is going to get in the way of having a nice evening out and enjoying each other's company, then I say forget the stupid diet."

"Can't we enjoy each other's company over broiled trout?"

"Not tonight."

At this point, what she wants and needs is support. Instead she's being sabotaged. If you were to ask her husband if he sabotaged his wife's diet, he would probably say, "No, I just wanted pizza." But his behavior was sabotage. He just didn't recognize it as such. Conscious or unconscious, however, his sabotage was effective.

I heard about one woman who was always trying to lose weight to please her husband. The marriage had many problems, and a divorce was initiated. During the separation, the couple became friends, in part because she went on a crash diet and lost the weight her husband had always complained about.

One night she came home and her husband was there at her place. Their relationship was beginning to show some promise again—until that night. She was on liquids (not an approved weight-loss method by my standards, but nevertheless, that is the truth of this story), but he was hungry. He wouldn't tempt her by asking her to join him in eating out. Instead, he cooked for himself a generous plate of bacon in the microwave. Her microwave, her apartment, her bacon. Of course he knew bacon was always her favorite food, especially when she was very hungry. Did he consciously mean to sabotage her diet? Conscious or not, he did.

Another woman's husband worked in a supermarket. He had access to broken or damaged cases of merchandise. At times he brought home whole cases of Snickers bars or chocolate chip cookies. He put them in the freezer with the comment. "These are for the kids."

This woman went about her daily routine. She cleaned, cooked and went to work. She came home after a trying day at the office, made dinner and, as she and her husband cleaned up the kitchen, she went to the freezer to store some leftovers. WHAM! she was confronted with 100 Snickers bars. However, she had just eaten and had the strength to close the door with a sigh of relief.

Later on in the week, she was home alone. She and her husband had been considering a major purchase. They had not agreed on the make or price of that purchase and had in fact argued almost continually for the last few days. When she was dealing with painful emotions, such as occurred when she fought with her husband, she was drawn to eat sweets. She didn't even realize it, but she was. One evening, she was sitting alone in the family room with a magazine on her lap. She was just looking at the pictures, not reading anything other than the headlines and perhaps the captions under the pictures. She was really processing the emotional pain of the past few days, even though she was not thinking specifically about it.

She turned a page of the magazine and a Snickers bar was attractively displayed. Without consciously making the decision, she walked to the freezer, opened the door and removed a three-ounce bar. In the kitchen she took a sharp knife, cut it with great precision into small, bite-size pieces. Arranging the wonderful confection on a small plate, she took it back into the family room. She repositioned herself on the sofa, picked up the magazine and, one by one, enjoyed the mouth-watering chunks—All 390 calories.

We might ask, "Did your husband sabotage your diet?"

"No, of course not," she defends. "He wasn't even here."

"Where did the candy come from?"

"My husband brought it home."

"Did having the Snickers bars there sabotage you?"

"Yes, but it's not my husband's fault."

"We are not placing blame on your husband, only identifying acts of sabotage. Did having the Snickers available to you sabotage your eating that evening?"

She sighs, "I'm really not very strong, am I?"

"That's not the point. Strong or weak is not the issue here. Were you sabotaged?"

She finally admits, "Yes, I was."

Does your husband *verbally* express a supportive attitude toward your weight loss and/or efforts to stop overeating? Then how do we understand his actions? How do we encourage his love and support toward his wife? How can this family reconcile the *desired* support with what is happening?

> Let your eyes look straight ahead, fix your gaze directly before you. Make level paths for your feet and take only ways that are firm. Do not swerve to the right or the left; keep your foot from evil. (Prov. 4:25–27)

> Cut through and make firm and plain and smooth, straight paths for your feet—[yes, make them] safe and upright and happy paths that go in the right direction—so that the lame and halting [limbs] may not be put out of joint, but rather may be cured. (Heb. 12:13, Amplified Bible)

This means we are to take definitive actions that will assure success. Remove from the cupboards, refrigerator and freezer all those items that would give you ammunition for failure within times of weakness and temptation. In effect, our friend should remove the candy bars from her freezer.

"But," you protest, "my husband and children expect to have candy available to them."

What would your husband do if you got rid of all sweets? Would he beat you? Would he pout and give you the silent treatment? Would he yell and throw things? Over what? No cake or cookies? Would he actually throw a temper tantrum over not having brownies or ice cream available to him every moment? If so, you need to have *him* read this book. (I think he should anyway.) If he is such a child that he stamps his foot and demands his own way over food, rather than sacrificing his desires for your good, he really needs to make some positive changes to improve your relationship.

Now there is another wrinkle when it comes to family sabotage. Sometimes a spouse can give a "double message"—that is, he can speak out of both sides of his mouth. Let me give you an example.

A husband asks his wife, "How about going out for Mexican food?"

"But, darling, you know that I am on a diet. Mexican food is one of the most tempting foods for me to overeat. Don't you want me to get thin?"

"Sweetheart, I love you just the way you are. You don't have to be thin for me."

And yet, every time they are at the beach, he can't keep his eyes off the pretty and slender women in their attractive bathing suits. And at church, she notices how friendly he is to all the slender women and how he ignores all the overweight ones—including her!

This is called a "double message." Double messages are hard to interpret because one message is sent by his words and another sent by his actions. They are hard to respond to because the one receiving the message doesn't know which one to believe. His words say, "I love you just the way you are." But his actions say, "But I really prefer to look at these women."

Many are sabotaged like this on an emotional level. A spouse may pick at an old wound through criticism, or tease about a sensitive issue. Maybe there are other relationship problems.

Maybe it's the issue of where to spend Christmas. Perhaps she is not comfortable with his family because of their conversation, or table manners, or the fact that she is the only fat sister-in-law in the entire clan. His mother doesn't hesitate to mention that at every opportunity with remarks like:

"I'm surprised that Joe married you. He never dated any other fat girls at all."

"Haven't you ever considered that my Johnny might find slender women a temptation?"

"Why don't you do something about your weight before it's too late?"

"I never knew anyone who carried all their weight in the rear before."

You ended up fighting about the holiday. You felt trapped, and you felt that he was being inconsiderate. You agreed to go just to end the conflict, but began to dread the visit, and your usual Christmas cheer died: *emotional sabotage*!

Sabotage is not an easy problem to deal with. It takes courage to face the issues, negotiate an agreement and stand your ground. Sometimes it will be painful. But the results will be worth all the effort.

Don't you dare, at this point, lay all the blame and responsibility on your family that you are fat! I am not saying that at all. What I *am* saying is, even though you make all the right efforts, join the right programs and read the right books, you might be experiencing sabotage.

But let me say one thing *loud and clear*. I do not believe that sabotage is an excuse to continue overeating! Rather, once you know what is happening, you have the knowledge that will help you resist. Someone else may be responsible for the sabotage, but *you* are responsible for your eating.

However, your family is intricately involved with your life. If you are overeating, they are involved to some degree in that behavior. If you want to stop overeating, they will be involved in that process as well. The family is a unit made up of its parts—the individual persons. Start looking at the problems of overeating as a *family problem*, and *family support* as part of the solution.

You need support, not double messages, not sabotage from your family to make the changes needed to stop overeating. This will mean changes in your family's way of doing things.

Let this realization sink in deep: In addition to understanding *how* they sabotage you, you need to also understand *why*. The answer is simple, but not easy. It is this: If your family is sabotaging your thinning process, they probably have an investment in keeping you fat, or at least in keeping you overeating.

This is what we must consider next.

THINK ABOUT IT

Is there a "Snickers bar" incident that you can remember in your own family?

Does your husband (wife, roommate) eat your favorite foods in front of you?

Does your family sabotage your weight management and/or disciplined eating efforts?

CHAPTER EIGHT

INVESTMENTS

The church is lovely with the flowers, ferns and candles all arranged expertly. The bridesmaids all look fresh and feminine, the groomsmen all formal and strong. The bride is radiant in her gown and veil. The groom is beaming and proud. The soloist has sung. Now, the vows:

> ". . . to have and to hold from this day forward, for better for worse, for richer for poorer, in sickness and in health, to love and to cherish, till death do us part, according to God's holy ordinance, thereto I pledge thee my faithfulness."

The minister's benediction is eloquent. The wedding is over: The marriage must begin.

My own wedding was a quieter affair, held in our pastor's living room on a Tuesday afternoon. But the vows and rings were exchanged and the minister said the eloquent benediction just as if we were in a cathedral.

We often think of weddings in terms of romance. But consider this for a moment. A wedding is much more than romance and wonder. It's the ceremony in which we make the most important and expensive investment of our entire lives. This is where we make promises that we expect to keep the rest of our lives. And this is where we are "promised to."

We are used to thinking of marriage in terms of commitment, but there is much more taking place. When we consider only commitment, we are looking at just one half of a double-sided issue. Investment is the other side of that issue.

We commit *to*. But we invest *in*.

Let's get a handle on what I am talking about when I use the word *investment*. In this book, the word can be used with either of two definitions in mind: First, the conscious or unconscious emotional dependence and need for security that one has for another is an investment; second, investment refers to those actions we take in an effort to protect our emotional interests.

In the husband/wife relationship the marriage is the initial investment (#1) that is made. From there, investments (#2) are made, actions are taken, things are done, in order to protect that investment.

The nursery rhyme, while silly, illustrates our point clearly.

Peter, Peter, pumpkin-eater,
    Had a wife (investment #1)
And couldn't keep her.

So he put her in a pumpkin shell
    (investment #2)
And there he kept her very well.
    (protecting investment #1)

Peter hadn't read this book, however, and didn't know how to *positively* protect and build up his investment in his wife.

In real life, things are different than Peter's experience, but for many the principle is the same. More about that later.

But back to our scenario of the wedding day for a moment.

The bride lovingly looks into her groom's eyes and promises to be everything she can possibly be to him for the rest of her life. In response he promises to be and do the same for her.

In one ceremony used many years ago there was a charge to the bride as follows:

> You assume grave responsibilities. He whom you are about to wed will look to you for solace in the hour of trial. Your smile should be his brightest day, your voice his sweetest music, your industry his greatest wealth, your economy his safest steward, your lips his faithful counsellor, and your prayers his most able advocate at heaven's court.

Quite a charge wouldn't you say? Quite an investment for a man to make in a woman! And what a commitment for a woman to make to a man! Yet, in spite of all the divorce statistics, the fact remains, people are still interested in the long-term benefits and personal returns gained through investing themselves in marriage.

In short, once married you have an investment to protect. Now this is where it gets sticky.

Florence Litthauer wrote a book aptly named, *After Every Wedding Comes a Marriage*. The title alone reveals wise counsel. Just as every serious investor looks after his interests in his investments, so do the marriage partners in their investment.

Let's go to Scripture to illustrate our point.

Matt. 25:14–18 tells the parable of the man who gave his servants some of his property before he went on a journey. One of the servants, who was given five talents, went immediately and invested the whole amount and was able to double it. The servant who was given two talents did the same, with the same result. But the man who was given only one talent "went off," the Bible says in verse 18, "dug a hole in the ground and hid his master's money."

The first two servants were more willing to take risks, and therefore were rewarded with a return. But the third servant was fearful and not willing to take risks, and kept the talent he had under cover. In the end, he had only what he started with, one talent. But the others had twice what they had in the beginning.

So it is with our marriages; some of us take the necessary risks and give each other space, encouragement and support as we grow and experience life together. Others of us are not secure enough in ourselves to take risks, so we tend to sabotage each other's efforts toward growth, independence and wholeness. This is all in an unconscious effort to protect our investment in the marriage.

However, the principle of this parable is true in our marriages as well. The one who continues to invest in life beyond the marriage, with the support and encouragement of his spouse, reaps so much more from the marriage. And the one who buries his investment finds out that he may be married, but often times doesn't have a real marriage.

Let me translate all that into practical illustrations. A man gets married and he wants his wife to stay faithful to him—like Peter, the pumpkin-eater. He can make several choices. Some are positive, and some negative. He can work on learning to communicate effectively with her, to listen to her feelings and opinions; he can find ways to express caring and support within the relationship; he can find ways to edify or build her up; he can develop good manners and helpful attitudes toward her and her concerns.

Or, as we consider the subject in this book, he might sabotage any efforts she makes toward losing weight—putting her in a "pumpkin shell," or at least making sure that she has opportunity to put herself in there!

Let's say that, in his mind, overweight women are not attractive, not appealing. To his way of thinking, overweight keeps her safe from the approach of other men. Sadly enough, this also makes her unattractive and unappealing to him as well, and begins to cause problems in the marriage. She decides that she wants to be thinner to please him. He agrees that he would indeed like it if she were thinner. So she goes to the "Free To Be Thin" class at church and takes the whole program seriously. She watches that she eats balanced, calorie-correct meals, no snacks; she regularly exercises and begins to make progress. He quietly goes along with her plan, maybe even supports it to some degree. He has to make little or no effort other than cooperating with the food choices she is putting on the table.

But . . . after ten or twenty pounds of weight-loss, some well-intentioned man comes up to her in church and says, within his hearing, "You're really looking terrific."

Whoa! Some alarms ring deep within his insecurities.

"Let's go out for dinner today," he says quickly.

She's not sure.

"I want to go to the smorgasbord," he says. Then he announces, with just a touch of firmness, "You may be on a diet, but I'm not. And I'm in the mood for an all-you-can-eat place. One that has great desserts."

The unconscious process of sabotage has begun.

The sabotage in this particular case comes from his need to feel more secure in his investment. Since he doesn't know how to positively reinforce his wife, to protect his investment, he ends up unconsciously sabotaging her. He does have other options, but they would involve effort on his part.

Another attempt at keeping her faithful may be a legalistic adoption of rigid rules concerning use of makeup, attractive hairstyles, flattering clothes, and so on. An unconscious attempt at making sure she is not pretty to other men. However, she ends up being very unattractive to him as well.

Then confusion sets in. Why is he not as attentive as he was when we were dating? Why doesn't he want me to buy perfume now that we are married when he always liked it before? Why does he pay more attention to the slimmer, more attractive women at church, even though he insists I don't have to put all that "garbage" on my face?

The temptation is to think that this is all the wife's responsibility, that she must try to make him feel more secure in the marriage. But in reality the problem is in him. He is trying to protect his investment. His methods may be totally inappropriate and unproductive while his motives could be right on target.

This process is not limited to the overeater, or the overweight person. It happens all the time in families everywhere. And it doesn't always happen with a man sabotaging his wife. It can work both ways. She might be the insecure one.

Let's imagine that a man has just been accepted in a graduate program that will most assuredly help him advance in his career. Let's say that his advancement will mean a nicer house in a better neighborhood. If she is insecure, his advancement, while being good news for him, is shaky news for her. She might be afraid that if he gets more education, the intellectual gap between them will be so wide that she will be left helplessly on the opposite side. At this point, she sees her investment threatened and needing protection. Her behaviors are probably unconscious. If they had another baby, he would not be able to afford his schooling. She gets a little careless, and also gets pregnant. And whether she *intended* to get pregnant or not, her investment has been protected.

One woman told me that she is really afraid of intimacy. Closeness in a relationship is very threatening, so she manages to keep extremely busy. She's the one who takes on every job and program at church. She is able to be around people a lot, but closeness is not usually found in a committee setting. She also discovered that her husband is not as interested in a physical relationship with her during pregnancy. So . . . you guessed it! One baby right after another.

Perhaps you think you know this woman— the one at your church or neighborhood Bible study who has six kids, stair-step fashion, is den mother, team mother, room mother, Sunday school teacher, choir member and car-pool organizer. Well, maybe you know her and maybe you don't. (Is she you?)

There are other choices our busy friend could make to protect her investment in her marriage.

On the positive side, she could get an outside job that would challenge and cause her to grow as her husband does. Perhaps it would be a good time for her to pursue her own education. She might need to see a counselor for a while and work through her fears and painful emotions.

On the negative side, she could insist that she is miserable in this city. She could cry and beg and make him so miserable he moves to another city to keep peace. Of course, to follow our story line on through, the new job and new house tie him down. Or maybe she doesn't do anything quite so drastic, she just charges so much that he has to take a part-time job to make the payments.

If she is also an overeater, eating to salve pain or conscience, she is probably gaining weight. This often adds to her feeling of inferiority and the whole cycle is reinforced many times.

Let me repeat, the problem is not really in the marriage, it is in her. But the way she brings it into the marriage is so subtle it often takes a professional counselor to help separate it all.

What about the husband who loves his wife so much that he would do anything to look better in her eyes? That is his way of protecting his investment in the marriage. He is sure that she could have done better and often tells her so.

How is a wife to answer that? "Yes, dear, I could have"—indicating that he really is a loser. Or, "No, dear, I couldn't have"—giving evidence that she really is a worse loser than he's already convinced he is.

Or he can put down her friends, trying to look better to her comparatively. But what really happens is that she is forced to look for more positive things in their defense. Her friends look better and better to her. And the opposite of what he was trying to accomplish occurs.

Or he could brag constantly, telling his wife how good he performs at work, while never offering to lift a hand around the house. This does not do much for her image of him. Telling her of the "babes" he dated before he got "shackled" to her doesn't help either.

Think about the following statements:

To avoid focusing on me and my problems

a. Let's focus on you and your problems.

b. I can contribute to your problems in a way that would make them seem worse.

c. Let's magnify your problems and blow them out of proportion.

d. Let's make you responsible for all our conflicts.

e. I can discourage communication on a

feeling level for fear of exposure.

f . I can hide my problems from you, with the result that you are obviously the only one with problems.

Do you feel the tension? This really happens in marriages. Not all, but some.

If a man wants to look better in his wife's eyes, nothing does it faster than for him to jump to her defense and support when she needs it. He doesn't need to call her friends on the carpet for treating her badly, but simply take her in his arms and reassure her. Or he can listen to her feelings, accepting them as honest. Realizing the privacy that she has trusted him with would do wonders in many marriages. Helping with the children, reading to them, playing with them is a positive, too. Nothing makes a man look taller to his wife than to see him being tender with their children. How masculine a man looks walking into a bedroom with a teddy bear or single rose in hand for his sick and recuperating wife.

However, there are many reasons why people use the same destructive techniques in handling their emotional investments as the servant in Matthew 25. They think their investment is safe, but the opposite is true.

Why don't people face this problem and deal with it directly? It may be because of fear. It can be because they fear that it could cost them too much emotionally, or be too difficult. Maybe they just don't know how. Perhaps, in the family system that taught them how to deal with painful emotions, they were taught to avoid difficult emotional adjustments. They could have been taught to hide their emotions and insecurities. Maybe they were taught that people who show emotions are unstable.

Why do we protect our emotional investments the way we do? Let's look again at the response of the servant who hid or buried his talent.

In Matt. 25:25, the servant says, "I was afraid."

Fear causes us to bury our investments instead of risk them.

Pride is another reason. Many of us are unwilling to be humble before our partners and admit that we are insecure. Perhaps we have fear mixed with our pride. We're afraid that he—or she—will love us less for our insecurities.

Yet Scripture teaches that humility is one of the most dynamic strengths of leadership. Matthew 18:4 says:

> Whoever humbles himself like this child is the greatest in the kingdom of heaven.

Likewise, Matthew 23:11–12 says:

> The greatest among you will be your servant. For whoever exalts himself will be humbled, and whoever humbles himself will be exalted.

Again, in James 4:6:

> God opposes the proud
>   but gives grace to the humble.

Our own carnal nature encourages us to behave in ways that are contrary to God's Word. But in addition to that very strong influence is the fact that in our childhood family, we were taught various ways to protect our investment. (It gets a little tangled here. But hang in there with me, OK?)

One way families teach children to handle emotionally painful events or subjects is simply to avoid them. When a man or woman senses that confronting issues will be uncomfortable, a natural inclination is to avoid it. When applied to the concept of investment in marriage, avoidance is the equivalent of digging a hole and burying the entire marriage. Not because they want to, but because they don't know anything else.

I have listed here for you a few common things that people try to avoid. (By the way, overeating is often simply a means of avoidance.)

failure

success

crisis

attractiveness

closeness

social pressure

confrontation

new situations

painful memories of the past

the unknown

These concepts are not limited to family situations. Friends and siblings also sabotage each other when they need support, for many of the same reasons marriage partners do. However, it is in the strong bond of marriage that the deepest investment is made, reflected in the marriage vows themselves. "Till death us do part" is both a strong commitment and a long investment!

This insight is to help you understand the investments you have made in your relationships, your marriage, and your children. Please don't take the attitude: "So that's what you are doing to me." That is blame. Rather, take the attitude: "So that's what's going on between us, preventing us from being to each other what we really need and want." That is identifying the problem. When we identify a problem we can begin to work on it together. Philippians has a wonderful model for exploring the investments couples have made to each other.

Philippians 2:1–4:

> If you have any encouragement from being united with Christ, if any comfort from love, if any fellowship with the spirit, if any tenderness and compassion, then make my joy complete by being like-minded, having the same love, being one in spirit and purpose. Do nothing out of selfish ambition or vain conceit, but in humility consider others better than yourselves. Each of you should look not only to your own interests [or investments], but also to the interests of others.

When we take this scriptural model as our

own, when we understand the intense and deeply personal investment we make in each other, sabotage will cease and support will begin.

We have given a good deal of time to looking at the sabotage your family may be directing toward you. But *you* may be sabotaging yourself as well. We will look at the issue of self-sabotage in the next chapter.

THINK ABOUT IT

Weigh all of what you have read here with the accurate scale of the Bible.

Apply that portion which applies to you.

Share this book with your spouse (or friend or sibling), and do not ask for a response right away.

Consider whether or not you and your partner could benefit from talking to a professional counselor or pastor.

Pray. Ask God for wisdom and strength as you dig up the investment from the hole it has been buried in and return to the spirit of love in which you initially made the investment.

CHAPTER NINE

SELF-SABOTAGE

In chapter seven we defined sabotage as "the behavior of one family member that discourages and/or undermines the efforts toward change in another."

Please understand that, in addition to sabotaging each other, people just as often sabotage themselves. Let's define "self-sabotage" as "the behavior of a person that discourages and/or undermines the efforts toward change in his own life."

Do you remember the lady with the freezer full of Snickers bars? Let's go back to her for a moment.

We saw that her diet efforts were sabotaged by the availability of the candy. We saw that since her husband had brought them into the house, her diet was sabotaged by him. But let's say that he wasn't the one who brought them home. Let's say *she* got them on sale because she knew that the grandchildren would enjoy them. She could have all kinds of conscious, even logical thoughts, all sorts of generosity to justify her purchase. But in a case like that, she has sabotaged herself.

When reading the rough draft of this chapter, a friend exclaimed, "Neva, right now I have sitting on the front of the main shelf of my refrigerator a huge potato salad that I made for my husband."

I looked up from my cross-stitching. "So?"

"Don't you see? I have enough of that potato salad to last several weeks! I plan to use it for his supper, and for him to take in his lunch."

"So?" I repeated.

She was getting very agitated. "It's a trap for me! I could have made a very small batch, just enough for supper with some left for his lunch tomorrow, but I didn't. I made much too much. If I don't eat some of it along the way, it will spoil. I am much too thrifty for it to go to waste."

I knew that with this revelation I was just along for the ride. No comment from me was really necessary.

"I have sabotaged myself. But because I made it 'for my husband,' I also deceived myself by blaming it on him." She grew thoughtful, with just a hint of being teary-eyed. "How many more times have I sabotaged myself, but blamed it on him?"

I couldn't answer that question for my friend, but I could guess that it will happen with less frequency from now on.

I've done it myself—bought too much candy

at Halloween and Easter, then appointed myself guardian of the goodies (to save their teeth)—only to steal from my own children!

I've made too many cookies at Christmas. One year I made several batches of that snack made with Chex cereals, nuts and pretzels. I intended to give it away as gifts in pretty Christmas tins, but changed my mind. I nibbled away, blissfully sabotaged by my *self*. I've bought things at the market "for the children," and then hidden them from them. I've bought things to keep for those occasions when company might come, only to discover it gone when the company arrived because I had eaten it. I've bought things, "for the freezer," as if the freezer were doing all the eating.

Did I mean to sabotage myself? Not consciously. But that was the end result. Even as I write this, I remember the shopping trip I made with my husband last week. I think of the food items in the kitchen, which I purchased and are not good for me to have around. When I point out the things that Lee adds to the shopping cart which sabotage my diet, he puts them back with a cooperative attitude. But what about those items he adds to the shopping cart that I do not comment about? And what about things *I* add to the shopping cart that sabotage me?

You see, even when you are aware of the process, unless you are committed to changing that process, it will continue. I have to make that commitment as much as you do. And it's not a commitment that is made once and for all; it is made daily, even momentarily, as I go through my routine activities as well as the unscheduled, unplanned activities I am confronted with continually.

Let's consider, for a moment, self-sabotage.

One question we asked in our research was, "What are your hobbies?" One hundred percent of the participants responded. But when we asked the question, "Can you see any positive effects for your being overweight?" Only twenty-five percent even attempted to answer the question. The rest left the question blank. We can only speculate why.

In one of our discussions, Dr. Dixon stopped for a moment and reflected. "It's not uncommon for my wife to ask me why I'm upset. I growl back at her that I'm not upset. I ask her why she would ask me that question and she says, 'Well, you're standing in front of the refrigerator with the door open, looking for something to munch on when you just finished dinner.' "

Dr. Dixon concluded, "We all can become emotionally dependent on food as a means to satiate our feelings. In other words, many people sabotage themselves with food instead of dealing with their feelings."

This is true with me sometimes, too. It happens so quickly.

In response to our questionnaire, we heard other reasons for self-sabotage:

"I see now that I used my overweight to hide from life. I am so heavy I don't have to make decisions to do things, because I cannot do them physically." When this woman loses weight, she will have to make those decisions. If she doesn't prepare herself for those changes, she will be setting herself up for sabotage.

"I'm very depressed when I am overweight," another woman responded. "When I am depressed I become introverted and want to stay home. Then I eat even more." This woman sets herself up by eating more to be able to have an excuse to stay home and eat even more.

"When I am disciplined in this area, I become disciplined in other areas." If being a disciplined person is not what I really want, then overeating is a way out. Being responsible and disciplined requires a bit of effort—too much effort for some.

"When I am near my goal weight I look so wrinkled and old." If a person cannot handle the aging process and its implications, one way to get rid of the wrinkles and what they represent is to fill them out by overeating and gaining weight.

"Being disciplined in my eating makes me face so many other areas of pain in my life that need to be cleaned up. When I can't face that, I eat."

"It [being overweight] gives me an excuse to do as little as possible because I am so tired and need to rest."

"I can use being overweight as an excuse for others not to expect so much from me."

There are more selfish reasons to stay overweight. These are the real reasons that people sabotage themselves.

Twenty-two percent of the people who answered this question said that being overweight is a protection for them in relationships with men.

"Men don't make as many advances toward me."

"It has protected me from difficult dating situations."

"I don't have to struggle with being sexually attractive to men."

"I don't have to deal with being propositioned and flirted with."

"I don't have to worry about a man falling in love with me."

"I don't have to worry about men trying to touch me."

These statements are indicators of underlying issues that need to be dealt with in a person's life before self-sabotage will end.

I am reminded of John 5:1–6, the story of the invalid who was by the pool of Bethesda for many years. It was the custom and belief of those in our story that if an angel stirred the waters of the pool, the first one in the water would be healed. This man had been waiting near the pool for that to happen.

Jesus approached him and challenged him with just a few direct words: "Do you want to be well?"

What a question! Wasn't the fact that the man was in the right place waiting for the right time enough evidence to indicate he wanted to be well?

I think perhaps the man was like many overeaters I know. They wait for a program to come to them, sort of like waiting for the angel to trouble the waters. And they have their excuses.

Sometimes we look at the commercials on TV and in magazines or newspapers and want to believe what they promise: If we could just go to one of the "weight loss" clinics and in six to ten weeks be thin and lovely! Then surely all our problems would go away.

So many people equate the solution to all of their other problems with their size or overeating. But the reverse may be true. The overeating may be a result of other problems.

You see, *thin* will not enable me to handle a critical mother-in-law. Thin will not bring back a rebellious run-away teenager. Thin will not stop a husband's roving eye. Thin will not solve the problems at church. Thin will not give you the "happy-ever-after" life you want. Getting thin will not solve all your problems or heal all your pain; but facing problems and pain in a healthy attitude might help you stop sabotaging yourself with food—and help you get thin.

Unless you have the courage to face and deal with the painful issues in your life, you may continue to set yourself up for sabotage. What's more, you may continue to blame those problems on the fact that you cannot control your eating or your weight.

If I went to the most effective weight-loss clinic in town, followed the program to the letter and lost weight, and if I didn't know about sabotage in the family and also how I sabotage myself, what good would it do? It would only start all over again.

In reading this chapter, listen to Jesus who says to you, "Do you really want to be well?"

THINK ABOUT IT

Can you identify some ways in which you are sabotaging yourself?

Do you blame most of your problems on being overweight?

Do you hide from your troubles by eating?

Do you blame acts of self-sabotage on your family?

CHAPTER TEN

CHANGING THE SYSTEM

W e have looked at the past family system to gain insight into the matter of emotions and overeating. How do we change our *present* family system so that our own families provide the support we need to accomplish growth and maturity?

I see so many people who go to support groups for a myriad of reasons. First they go to this diet group, then to a clinic specializing in weight loss. When that doesn't work, they go to the dentist to wire the jaws shut or to a surgeon to staple or band the stomach. When the wires come off or the surgical procedure causes severe physical trauma, then what? There have even been support groups established for surgical weight-loss patients. There are groups everywhere.

I want to yell, "Stop! What about your family as a support group?"

You may be thinking, "Sure, Neva, sure." But I am serious. Making a few changes in your family system may be all it takes for your family to become a welcome source of support and a means to end the sabotage. In some ways the changes themselves will be so healthy that your overeating may be checked or controlled without ever dealing with it directly. In other cases, changing the family into a validating supportive group, may give your family the assistance they have been looking for in order to help you lose weight and/or stop overeating.

My family had been openly supportive of my dieting, but none of us recognized the ways their support was sabotaged—sometimes with food, but frequently by covert ways our system had of undermining all of us emotionally.

As I told you in the first part of this book, I was faced two years ago with having by-pass surgery reversed, knowing I was going to have a period of certain weight gain. I also knew that to lose weight again would be many times harder than ever before. In addition, my work has become the major source of our income. I had once joked that if I was ever to "lose my job," it would be because I had gained weight. I was terrified of the future. I was scared to death! I needed my family's support more than ever before.

We have had to make changes in our family system to allow me to talk about my painful feelings and fears. We made adjustments to our system to make it safe for me to talk about my weight. My husband has never once complained about the weight I have gained. Instead, he has tried to see the pain from my perspective. My family has become a support group for me.

My husband has also taken up a regular routine of exercise and, even though he does not pressure me, he invites me to join him. He provides me with a gentle reminder through example in this area.

My son and husband are also sensitive to me when I tell them I can't handle eating at a certain restaurant.

Through daily, disciplined accountability and maintaining a quality quiet time with the Lord, I have learned how to have victory over discouragement about my weight. The depression that threatened to overtake me, destroy my work and negatively affect my family has lifted in large part. I am able to stick to a controlled, healthy eating plan. I am exercising more regularly. We have taken steps to make more room for sharing feelings, goals, dreams and fears. I am now free to say, "I can't have that (food) in the house; it sabotages me."

Why? How? Because we made changes in the way we operate as a family.

When you read chapters four and five, did you recognize destructive patterns in your childhood family system? Have you carried any over into your present family? Make the decision to break destructive patterns from your past and reinforce the good patterns your parents handed down along with the negatives ones.

Are you repeating your parents' mistakes?

Are you a critical family?

Are you able to share your emotions, both happy and sad?

Are you able to share your fears and hopes with your family?

Is there room given for each member to explore his painful feelings and discover help for them?

Are you teaching your children to cope—or cover?

Do you see your adolescent children as people going through a painful time, or do you see yourself as the unfortunate parent of adolescents? If you can see the pain your children have, they can probably talk and share this pain with you. If the latter is the case, they are probably handling their pain in other ways, such as stifling it or talking to their friends. Maybe they are taking drugs, or, in many cases, overeating.

Do you want your family to change? It will take some time, so don't give up. But persevere. The results will be wonderful.

Changes in the family system begin when we first admit to ourselves and to each other that the way we are handling things isn't working. Even admitting that much may be a drastic change and cause your family members to "dig in" in defense. But be determined. Repeat it again in a little while if you don't find openness. Explain to your spouse and children that what you are doing doesn't work. The present system doesn't meet the need to help all of you handle your emotions in a constructive way.

What you are doing now may have been effective in the past, but as your needs change be flexible enough to make changes in your family system to meet these changes.

Ecclesiastes 3:1, 3 says it this way:

There is . . . a time to tear down
and a time to keep.

Your needs change as you grow. Your family's needs change as they grow. The system must change to meet these changing needs. Don't keep an old system beyond its time.

I sat with a group of overweight women who happened to be Christians and discussed changes that they would like to see in the relationships they had with their husbands. One said with tears, "I would like to be able to tell my husband when I am having a hard time with my eating."

Another said, "I would like to be able to tell my husband how much I weigh and share with him my desire to be at goal weight."

"Why can't you?" I asked.

They all seemed surprised at the question and admitted to me that they could not be totally honest with their husbands. Why couldn't this group of Christian wives be honest?

We explored the subject further. I asked them to define honesty, and together they agreed on a definition: "Honesty is being straight with another."

A simple uncomplicated definition, they all said. But impossible to accomplish in their marriages unless major changes were made.

Through the conversations I had with them, I discovered something worth sharing with you.

Somehow these women had taken on the total responsibility for the atmosphere of their home. One had decided that she was not going to be the contentious woman mentioned in Prov. 25:24, no matter what the cost. She had worked so hard at doing everything and being everything she could for her husband that she had no person left inside.

One told me she had decided that all the changes needed were in her. If her husband hurt her, she had to be stronger. If she was disappointed by his forgetfulness, she needed to be less selfish. If she felt shut out when he ignored her, she needed to learn to be more fun to be with. If he paid her no attention, she felt it was up to her to change, to be more attractive, to do something worthy of his attentions.

Another said that she was afraid he only married her to have an outlet for his sexual desires. When I questioned her, she said that the only time he was warm was at bedtime; the rest of the time he was private, cool and distant. It did not occur to her that he needed to change, only that maybe she needed to be warmer and more attractive to him. She did not see his responsibility to communicate; she thought that it was her responsibility to draw him out.

All of these women saw changes that needed to take place in their family systems. Honesty was sadly lacking in each case.

I posed the following unfinished sentence and asked each one to fill in her own ending: "It is hard for me to be honest with my husband because—"

These are their responses:

It is hard for me to be honest with my husband because—

"I think I might be misunderstood and will be asked to explain, when I can't explain, only report my feelings."

"It might hurt his feelings."

"Based on past attempts at honesty, I could be presented with a list of grievances from him that he has saved for such an occasion as this. In other words, he never shares his complaints about me unless I share one or two about him. Then I get the 'you're-not-so-perfect-either' routine."

" 'Straightness' sometimes causes withdrawal, and it hurts me when he withdraws."

"He pouts."

"He avoids or drops people who have hurt his feelings in the past and refuses to work out issues with them, and I don't want him to drop me."

"He doesn't want to work things through, just takes the time to get over it." (I asked this woman what she did while he was "getting over it. You guessed it: she ate.)

"His response is usually negative."

"He doesn't want to be bothered."

"I don't want to be told, 'You shouldn't feel like that.' "

"I don't want to be talked down to."

"I'm afraid of stepping out of line."

"It's not a submissive thing to do."

"His ego is too fragile."

"It's easier not to be."

"He puts me down."

"He makes me feel that anything I have to say about a subject is not important."

"My problems are not regarded as his problems."

"I don't want to add to the load he already carries."

Then there was the surprising response we all could identify with:

"It is hard for me to be honest with my husband because when he responds the way he does to my honest feelings and hurts, it makes me face the fact that there are many things about him that I don't like and I don't want there to be any things about him that I don't like (the Prince Charming Syndrome).

Then I posed another fill-in sentence to the group, and got the following responses:"I can be honest with my husband when—"

"He's in a good mood." (I was taught that a good wife steps around her husband, not on him.)

"He's feeling good about himself." (I was taught that I am to build him up, make him feel like Mr. Wonderful, even if he is acting like the Incredible Hulk.)

"He's had a good day at work." (But what about my day at work?)

"I'm feeling good about myself." (Which is rarely.)

"I don't care anymore." (And then, what's the point. Things could get better through honesty, but by then "who gives a rip?")

"I don't feel that I have anything to lose." (And by then I'd rather be with someone else.)

I asked, "What do you do when you want to be honest and feel that you can't?"

"I protect him from the truth, even if it means I lie."

"I end up manipulating him, and others too."

"Cry."

"Cover up my feelings."

"I try to ignore the real issues."

"Eat."

"Spend money."

"Talk to my friends."

"I end up mothering him."

"I fantasize about another man. Perhaps what I would do or whom I would marry if he died."

"Pretend."

"Find other interests to take up my time."

"Focus on building relationships with my kids; they respond in ways that make me feel better about things."

The alternative used to help deal with the emotional pain caused by the lack of honesty and closeness in the marriages of these women is more threatening to the family than if she would simply pursue the problem with her husband. However, that threat is not as painful as the rejection.

The husbands need to do some changing, that is obvious. But so do the wives. Each needs to effect a positive wonderful change—a change that would come through finding the courage to be honest. The system needs changing.

Remember, I was only discussing these issues with women. I am sure that if I were with a group of men, the subject might have been another, but the issue the same: Changes needed in the family system.

So how does a person go about changing the system. How do we stop doing one thing and start doing another?

First review the chapter on forgiveness and apply the principles there to the present system as well as the past one. Unforgiveness only binds the family to the current way of doing things. Author Dan Betzer said, "By an act of your determined will, you decide to put the past with all its mistakes, fiascoes, and disasters behind you." That means your recent past as well as the distant past.

In addition, consider these suggestions:

Identify the problem; do not blame a person.

The difference is found in simply stating the problem in nonidentifying, or nonblaming terms. One could say, "There is a lack of honesty in our marriage," instead of, "You won't let me be honest."

Approach the problem; do not attack a person.

"Honey, I feel there is a lack of honesty in our relationship that we could work on," instead of, "You never let me be honest; you never want to hear my feelings."

Explore alternatives.

Together, think of ways that could make

room in your relationship for honesty. Brainstorm. Make a list of all the ways in which you could be honest with each other. Even the craziest idea is allowed.

Make decisions by consensus.

Discuss each suggestion on the list and tell how each of you would feel if that was the means by which you were to allow more honesty in the relationship. Then vote. The one item that comes closest to being first choice for both of you is the decision. Then stick to it.

What you have done is face the problem; you have chosen a constructive way to deal with the lack of honesty in the relationship, instead of overeating to compensate for the resulting bad feelings.

The lack of honesty is only used as an illustration here. There might be other things in your family that need changing. What are they?

Being able to share your emotions—hopes, dreams, fears, failures.

Being free to respond to each other without condemnation.

Sabotage.

One lady said to me, "I would like us to pray together about meaningful and personal issues without embarrassment or intimidation."

Another woman responded with, "I'd just like us to pray together. Period."

Sure, you might get some complaints and objections. But keep in mind that whenever there is change, there will probably be resistance first. Don't let the resistance discourage you to the point of giving up. Your marriage is worth it. You are worth it. Your family is worth it.

Michael Slater writes, in *Stretcher Bearers*:

> As Christians, we have a new life in Christ. His life within us is not to be separate from our relationships with one another. On the contrary, we are called to support these relationships in a new and better way. We need other people and we are meant to encourage one another. Every day we face difficulties and problems that require solutions. Some situations are harder than others, but life calls us to resolve them on a daily basis.[1]

There will be no way for you to make it if you choose to go through life's situations and struggles setting yourself apart from others. And your family can be the most important and significant "others" in your life. You need people who can touch you in positive ways, and your family can be taught to do that. You can also learn to be that positive support for them as well.

We are all capable of building love relationships free of negativity, sabotage and dishonesty. But we must put ourselves forward in positive commitment toward our future and forgiveness for the past.

You can become a family that encourages

and stands by each other no matter what the difficulty or situation. You can be people who allow each other to be real. You will be able to take off your masks. God will work in the lives of your family members so that they can accept you for who you are. Life's struggles will only bond you together tighter, not drive you apart.

You can become a Christian family in every sense of the word.

THINK ABOUT IT

Why not adopt this prayer as the prayer for your family?

> *Teach us to know*
> *   how much we need each other.*
> *Help us learn how*
> *   to be sensitive to each other*
> *   and open and accepting of each other.*
> *Thou who has brought the life of God to bring us*
> *   together—*
> *may our fellowship be the fellowship*
> *   of the Father*
> *   the Son*
> *   and the Holy Spirit. Amen.*[2]

NOTES

1. Michael Slater, *Stretcher Bearers* (Regal Books, 1985).
2. Reuben Welch, *We Really Need Each Other* (Zondervan Publishing House, 1982).

CHAPTER ELEVEN

WALKING IN LOVE

A story is told of a minister who stood beside a grieving husband at the grave of his wife. Those who had gathered for the funeral and burial service were leaving, and the minister took the arm of the widower. "It's time to go," he said gently.

"But you don't understand," the saddened man objected. "I loved her."

"I know," the minister assured him. "I appreciate the fact that you loved her, but now there are people waiting. It's time to go."

"No, you don't understand," the man repeated. "I loved her—and once I almost told her so."

Which carries the deepest regret: Something we did and cannot undo? or something left undone until it's too late to do?

Woman's Day magazine did a survey and published the findings in the November 11, 1986 issue. The question was asked, "Would you marry your husband again?" Fifty percent said they would, thirty-eight percent answered a definite no, and twelve percent said they weren't sure.

Furthermore, fifty-three percent said they felt like a partner to their husbands, thirty-nine percent felt like his housekeeper, twenty-seven percent said they felt like his mother and only twenty-eight percent said they felt like his lover.

A sampler I saw hanging on a wall reads: "To Love and Be Loved Is the Greatest Joy on Earth." But how many really know that joy? How many actually walk and lie together in true love? Let's look at this from a slightly different point of view than perhaps you have before.

A serious investor with considerable capital to lose reads the *Wall Street Journal* and other investment reports daily. He watches trends and looks for signs in the economy. He listens to economists and financial advisors. Why? Because the entire reason for investing is to get a good return on his investment.

Yet the same man who is tremendously astute in his business dealings can totally ignore the heaviest emotional investment he has ever made: his marriage.

If he sees that some of his stocks are slipping and reads that some of the companies he invested in are in trouble, he is likely to sell out and invest that money somewhere else.

Yet the same man can be losing ground in his emotional investment, his marriage. "Throwing good money after bad," as it were—not really getting a good return on the relationship, but continuing the same practice, the same patterns.

If you have discovered, through this book, ways in which your family system is shaky, don't throw it over for another. Just make some changes and discover how to invest in your relationships within your family so that you all get a good return for your investments.

For instance, take the issue of weight control and the involvement of the family in that effort. Have you been sabotaged by a husband (or mother or roommate) who says he wants to help you stem overeating and its effects in your life? Then approach him with the investment example. Let him see that to sabotage you emotionally or with food also sabotages his own investments.

We could talk about practicals here, and will a little later on in the text, but first let's identify that the real issue is not helping or hindering your eating plan and program. The real issue here is love. A relationship is based and flourishes on love.

Love attracts; love woos; love extracts promises; love blossoms. And love grows stale. Then, given the right moment, the right atmosphere, it begins again and love attracts once more. The wooing begins, promises are made, love blossoms and before you know it, grows stale again. Up and down go the emotions. Love is cyclic. I have been married to my husband for nearly twenty-five years, and I have fallen in love with him over and over again. So what happens in between times?

During the times we are not "in love"?

A marriage is not held together by romantic love. No. It's not.

"But," you may protest, "I do love my husband!"

Yes, and I love mine. But for us there have been days that we loved, but were not "in love."

The difference? Commitment.

If you draw circles in a row, with a little space between, and let them represent the times you were especially tender toward your marriage partner, then what hangs those times together? What keeps you from bailing out of the relationship when you don't feel like you are "in love"?

Take that same illustration that you just drew and connect those circles together with a line. It becomes like a string of pearls. The connective material, the substance that holds the relationship all together between the "in love" times is commitment.

If you can see that it takes the strength of commitment to hold together the preciousness of love, you will have come far in securing your marriage, your friendships and important relationships. Marriage is God's idea. Relationships are His design. He gave us the emotions and attractions to draw us together and the principles of commitment to keep us together.

Pastor Ed Tedeschi of St. Paul, Minnesota, said to me, "The implication is clear. The Lord doesn't expect any of us to be loners. It is His idea that we work together, worship together, encourage one another. We really do need each other."[1] I would add, it is also God's idea that we live together, be committed to each other, and grow as we face life's challenges together.

And yet there are stresses within the home, where people are living together, found in no other relationships.

The home is the logical place to begin a course in learning agape love.

> As Dr. Lovett has said, "Marriage and the home is the center of all life on earth. . . . It is a complete laboratory with all of the stresses and strains, trials and pressures packed under one roof. . . . Everything needed to produce Christlikeness in us can be found in the home." In other words, the home is a microcosm or miniature world, a facsimile of the world at large. The home, with its environment of stress and strain, is the best place to learn agape love.[2]

Just living together is a stress! How much more so when one is criticizing the other. When the husband tells the wife that she is ugly and unsightly because she is overweight, how is she supposed to respond when he is interested in lovemaking? When a wife tells her husband he doesn't look right, or his manners are awful, how is he going to feel when she suggests a dinner out at a very nice restaurant?

When the mate is compared to one's co-workers in appearance and comes up lacking, is it any wonder he refuses invitations to company parties and picnics with coldness?

What is the answer? Simply this: It is not enough for a couple to "be in love" when they marry; they must walk in love throughout the course of their marriage.

We may be living in the same apartment, or condo or ten-room house, but are we walking in love, allowing our relationships to grow?

For example, consider this conversation:

"I'm too fat!" a wife wails, looking in the mirror.

"Why don't you do something about it then?" inquires her husband.

Here is a perfect opportunity for a wife to let her "mask fall" and share with her husband the real reason behind her overweight. If it is overeating, she may tell him that some of the food he brings into the house is sabotaging her. She might tell him her fears and open up to him in honesty, sharing herself emotionally. She might find a critic. She might find a sympathetic listener and encourager. Her past experiences with her husband and former attempts at openness will affect her choice.

If the couple has made a commitment to walk in love, the husband might reach out to her and simply address her discouragement, trying to bring her some hope. He could say, "Come here, let me hold you. I know what it is like to face discouragement. It's not the end of the world. I love you. I'm here and you can count on me. Is there anything I can do to help you? Is there anything I need to stop doing to help you?"

By taking the focus off "fat" for a moment and by using this as an opportunity to grow closer will do more for helping a wife stay on her diet than will criticism.

Getting closer has its pain, however.

Paul told us to "carry each other's burdens" (Gal. 6:2). As we do this, we cannot help but feel what others are feeling. You may not hurt to the degree of intensity of the person who is hurting, but more times than not you will be hurting right along with that one.

Let's look at 2 John, verses 5 and 6:

> I am not writing you a new command but one we have had from the beginning. I ask that we love one another. And this is love: that we walk in obedience to his commands. As you have heard from the beginning, his command is that you walk in love.

A walk of love. A deliberate plan and program of walking in loving ways and attitudes toward each other. Wanting for each other success over temptation, victory over destructive habits and patterns. Think about:

> Husbands who will give their wives room to be less than perfect, but love beyond measure.

> Wives who will set their priorities and attitudes according to God's Word and respect their mates.

Husbands who will become so secure in Christ that if his wife loses fifty or a hundred pounds, he shares her victory instead of being threatened by it.

Wives who will stop martyring themselves in ways that are sabotaging to the entire system of the family.

Husbands who stop sabotaging their wives emotionally and with food in an effort to "keep her in a pumpkin shell."

Walking in love means living together according to God's Word.

Therefore let us stop passing judgment on one another. Instead, make up your mind not to put any stumbling block in your brother's [or wife's, or husband, or child's] way. As one who is in the Lord Jesus, I am fully convinced that no food is unclean in itself. But if anyone regards something as unclean, then for him it is unclean. If your brother [or wife, or husband, or child, or friend] is distressed because of what you eat, you are no longer acting in love. Do not by your eating destroy your brother [or wife, or husband, or child, or friend] for whom Christ died.

Let us therefore make every effort to do what leads to peace and to mutual edification. Do not destroy the work of God for the sake of food. . . .

It is wrong for a man [person] to eat anything that causes someone else to stumble. It is better not to eat meat or drink wine or to do anything else that will cause your brother [or

wife, or husband, or child, or friend] to fall.
(Rom. 14:13–15, 19–21)

Walking in love, according to God's Word,
means giving up what you would like to eat if it
would tempt someone else to eat what they think
they should not.

Translated into our daily lives, it means: *Husbands,* if your wife says she cannot handle the
pizza parlor tonight, go where there is a salad bar
instead; walk in love with her. *Wives,* if your husband has a spending problem, don't encourage
him to use his credit cards excessively to keep you
happy with "things." Love him without things.

Paul Bilheimer says,

> Antagonism toward a mate is first of all antagonism toward God. Lack of love for a marriage partner is really lack of love for God.
> "Beloved, let us love one another; for love is
> of God; and every one that loveth is born of
> God and knoweth God. He that loveth not
> knoweth not God. . . . If we love one another,
> God dwelleth in us, and his love is perfected
> in us. . . . If a man says, I love God, and hateth his brother [or mate] he is a liar: for he
> that loveth not his brother [mate] whom he
> hath seen, how can he love God whom he
> hath not seen?" (1 John 4:7–8, 12, 20)[3]

And I say, "Husbands, love your wives, just
as Christ loved the church and gave himself up
for her. . . ." How did Christ give himself up for
the church? He died for her. Can a husband say

he is giving himself up for the good of his wife when he insists that she cook fattening foods that she can't resist?

Phil. 2:4 says: "Each of you should look not only to your own interests, but also to the interests of others." This is walking in love.

Husbands,

Your attitude should be the same as that of
    Christ Jesus:
Who being in very nature God,
did not consider equality
    with God something to be
    grasped,
but made himself nothing,
    taking the very nature of
    a servant,
being made in human
    likeness.
And being found in
    appearance as a man,
He humbled himself
and became obedient to
    death—
even death on a cross!
    (Phil. 2:5–8)

Do you remember the story in Mark 2 about the four men who carried their friend on the stretcher to Jesus? It is a wonderful concept of marriage and the family as designed by God. Only when you can place your family in the story, each member at one of the corners of the stretcher, and one of you on it, can you begin to see the miraculous potential of your family as you learn to help each other.

There are steps that you can take to begin to walk in love:

Communicate: Tell your spouse of your desire to have a more loving and considerate relationship.

Negotiate: Discuss what that will mean to each of you in terms of the changes you each need to make and the masks you need to drop. Talk about the risks this means to each of you.

Appreciate: Find things about each other that you sincerely like and enjoy. Verbally express your appreciation.

Reciprocate: This is a give-and-take situation. Expect that you will have to do some changing as well as your partner. Be open to growth in both of you—your relationship and your family.

Determine as a family to walk in love. To be loving toward each other in understanding ways, considering each others' strengths and weaknesses. Finally, walk in honesty, allowing each other to share fears, tender spots and struggles.

THINK ABOUT IT

Do you want to help your husband or wife lose weight?

Do you want your husband or wife to be more understanding of how he/she sabotages you?

Do you see it's not enough to love each other, or to be in love with each other, but to walk in that love?

NOTES

1. Ed Tedeschi, pastor, Summit Avenue Assembly of God, St. Paul, Minnesota.
2. Paul E. Billheimer, *Don't Waste Your Sorrows* (Minneapolis: Bethany House Publishers, © Christian Literature Crusade, 1977), p. 88.
3. Paul Billheimer, op. cit., p. 90.

THINK ABOUT IT

Perhaps more questions have been asked than answered.

Dr. Dixon and I anticipated that very thing as we researched this book. Maybe you have thought, "My family doesn't sabotage me." Or "I'm not aware of my family playing a part in my overeating." How about, "My husband (or parent, or sister or child) wouldn't do anything except help me if I really wanted to diet." But now you are not so sure.

To help you see if some changes need to occur in your own family, ask yourself these questions, and honestly evaluate whether or not your family system could do with some alterations.

Does your spouse (parent, sibling, child, roommate, or friend):

Tease you?

Pressure you about your weight?

Admire others who are thinner in a way that you would notice?

Suddenly take an interest in cooking when you are dieting?

Offer you food that you should not eat while you are in a weight-control program or thinning process?

Offer you sympathy when you are discouraged?

Know about your feelings?

Show sensitivity toward your emotionally painful areas?

Listen to you when you need to talk?

Demand you fix food you cannot eat?

Stay with you during kitchen cleanup?

Understand you?

Really know you?

Walk or exercise with you?

Help with the children?

Share his/her feelings with you?

Hide things from you?

Eat after meals in front of you?

Eat food you cannot have in front of you?

Treat you as an equal?

Verbally express affection?

Love you?

About two years ago, Dr. Dixon called to my attention that Overeaters Victorious was limited in its ministry because we were approaching weight loss as if it were entirely an isolated individual problem. It is not.

Most who have lost weight and gained, lost and gained, have suspected there was a family connection, but have not had the insight into solving this most unsettling mystery.

Now you are aware of the family as a system. Since you are more aware of the possibilities of the support available from your family, you now know how to better approach your spouse for the help you need.

I can't begin to tell how much this new insight meant to me in my own personal life. It showed me where I needed to plug into my family more for the help I need. I saw that this was not a problem I had to carry alone. I realized in full force just how much I was dependent on my family and how much they are dependent on me. I came to understand the concept of interdependence within the family in a new and real way. I also saw the enemy's attack on that process. I could see how subtle attacks were going unnoticed, while all the time doing great damage. A whole new realm of understanding was right at my fingertips.

One of the major changes in my family system has been that before I started writing and working at home, the children always had immediate access to me. There was never a closed door, with me on one side and them on the other, unless I was in the bathroom. In an emergency, even that door was opened. But now I go to my study, put a "Do not disturb" sign on the knob and they have to respect it. They are older now, but they were used to constant access to Mom, and it took some adjustment in our system for me to be able to work and meet deadlines and schedules. They had to get over feeling left out, and I had to get over feeling guilty. But we've managed very well by changing our system through open communication.

Another change we have had to work on concerns an image of what it means to be a wife, an image I carried over from my parents and their family system.

I always felt that when a husband is home, he is his wife's first priority. I set everything else aside to attend to his needs and comfort. When he went to work I was free to pursue my work and interests. But when he was at home, I really tried to reserve the time just for him. Sounds ideal, doesn't it? But some of my worst times of feeling rejected by him came when he wanted to do something by himself. Then I had empty time, time to feel neglected and rejected.

And then he retired—but I didn't. *I* was just coming into my own in my speaking and writing, and he was home all the time. If I went to my office, I felt I should be home; if I stayed home to work, I felt I should be available to him. There were some very awkward adjustments to be made, and sometimes they were made with tears as I gave him some space and myself some freedom to do my work without guilt.

Our needs were changing, our system had to change as well. The discovery I made in these painful changes was that what was good for me was also good for him. He doesn't want me hovering over him; he also needed the space.

The three musketeers had the saying, "One for all and all for one." But when we have as our motto "What's best for all and all for the best," we sometimes have to let go of each other and give one another some space, or make a personal sacrifice for one another.

Even at the writing of this book, I see the changes occurring in my own family and feel the effect of the changes that have already been started and that are being put into place. I have recognized that my family is always changing—that's the way families are—but now we are changing under guidance, under our control, with our needs being met. We are adjusting to these changes and with every change that I want to see for my own needs to be met, my husband is finding the freedom to share with me the changes he also wants in order to have his needs met. It is truly an exercise in walking through interdependence. It is strengthening our relationship and deepening our commitment. We have not yet totally succeeded, but we have more hope than we have experienced in a long time. We are changing the way we do things to a more constructive, mutually edifying manner and are being drawn closer than ever before to each other and to the Lord.

This book is a continuation of my own dedication to the purpose of freeing those under condemnation, those struggling, those questioning and especially those hurting because of overeating behavior and/or being overweight. This has been a desire carried in my heart and prayers for some time. Dr. Dixon has shared that desire with me and has been an invaluable source of encouragement, strength and information. Together we trust God for His anointing as we have transferred this material to paper. It is our desire that this book glorify God and set more of His people free in this troubling and painful area.

I think I know overeating and/or overweight women enough to make the following statement: Overweight women all over the world, if they could join their voices together in one mighty chorus, would say:

> We need you, husbands. You are essential to our success. We need you to pray, love, sacrifice, encourage and support us. We need you to think about whether or not you have an investment in our being overweight. We both need to be aware of our changing needs and to help with modifying the family system to help meet those needs. Without you, the other part of me, I cannot make it. Are you with me in this, or are you going to be a part of my problem?

Let us ask you a question, husband, and pretend for a moment it is your wife asking it: "If I wasn't fat, how would that affect our family?

Perhaps you are not an overweight person, but are an overeater just the same and you have read this book for some additional insight into your problem. I hope the material covered here has been of real help to you. Please realize that I am sensitive to those of you who are trapped by overeating behavior, and yet for one reason or another do not get fat. I understand the pain you bear as a result of that lack of self-control. Whether you are an overweight overeater, or a slender one, apply the principles presented in this book to your life.

Maybe you are someone who has an overweight relative or friend and you have read this book to gather some insight as to how you can help them. Maybe as a result of reading this book you are more aware of how you can help your spouse while they are in their thinning process. I commend you on your commitment and tell you to hang in there in love and support. Your friend/spouse needs you and I trust that this book has given you what you need to be more of a support than ever before.

My pastor, Dr. Ray Frank, has said many times in his classes at church, "It is not important that you agree with me. It is important that you learn something." One time, while substituting for him, I reversed the statement and said to the class, "It is not important you learn something; it is important that you agree with me." That got a laugh, but surely made Pastor's point even stronger. I have to admit that I would like everyone who reads this book to agree with everything we have presented here, but I know that is not, in reality, going to happen. But my sincere hope is that as you have honored me with your time and the attention it has taken to read this book, your reward will be added insight.

My prayer, along with Dr. Dixon's, is that you will have the courage to take a look at these difficult issues and ask God for His strength and wisdom to recognize the principles of the family system and its effect on your own situation.

Perhaps you are one of those who doesn't have any chance at all of seeing a positive change in your family system. Maybe this book has only heightened your awareness of how much your family does not meet your needs and instead of feeling helped, you feel all the more alone. But you see, being aware of where the sabotage comes from offers strength to withstand it. Knowing you will not get help is far better than hoping you will somehow get it and never having it come through for you. It may not be the easiest thing to face, but if you will, you can then turn to Jesus for the help you need so desperately.

For the system to change, it needs only one member to change. The acts of sabotage may not stop, but you can stop being sabotaged. When that happens the system changes. With or without the help and cooperative attitudes of anyone else.

How do you begin?

Recognize acts of sabotage.

Remove yourself from the scene if possible. Walk out of the room. Take a drive. Go take a bath. But get away from the act of sabotage.

If the sabotage is food, remove the food. Grind it in the garbage disposal. Make the saboteur eat it—right then.

Confront the saboteur. Make sure that you attack the act of sabotage, make it clear what it means to you and stand your ground. Accept the person; reject the act.

Recognize that your eating may not be a character flaw at all. It may not be that you are undisciplined. It may not be that you are a glutton. It may simply be the way your family works. If that is the case, then a change in the way your family works is in order.

I invite you to think about and explore ways of bringing about the changes necessary to your own family system to help you with your own overeating and/or weight-loss changes. Some areas you might consider are:

Counseling with your pastor or a professional Christian counselor; talking with your spouse, with your family; joining or beginning an Overeaters Victorious group, sharing these insights with others who are also seeking answers.

I face a lifetime of responsible eating and weight management. Perhaps there will be the reward of weight loss for me. But maybe not. It is in God's hands entirely. If it were not for knowing that we have made such positive changes in the way our family works, I don't think I would have the courage to even try. But since I have learned these principles, I do try, every day. It's so much easier to face this problem when I know I am not alone.

A PERSONAL WORD FOR HUSBANDS

Ephesians 5:25–30 says:

Husbands, love your wives, just as Christ loved the church and gave himself up for her to make her holy, cleansing her by the washing with water through the word, and to present her to himself as a radiant church, without stain or wrinkle or any other blemish, but holy and blameless. In this same way, husbands ought to love their wives as their own bodies. He who loves his wife loves himself. After all, no one ever hated his own body, but he feeds and cares for it, just as Christ does the church—for we are members of his body.

With that scriptural admonition in mind, consider the following:

A study done at Brown University/Butler Hospital in Providence, Rhode Island, evaluated the influence of spouse cooperativeness and couples training in the treatment of obesity.[1] Twenty-nine obese men and women were assigned to three experimental conditions.

1. Cooperative spouse-couples training: Spouses were trained in modeling, monitoring, and reinforcing techniques.

2. Cooperative spouse-subject alone: Subjects attended meetings alone even though their partners had agreed to become involved in treatment.

3. Noncooperative spouse: Subjects had spouses refusing to participate in the program, and attended the sessions alone.

Result: At the three-month and six-month maintenance assessments, subjects in the spouse-couples training (group 1) lost significantly more weight than subjects in the other two conditions. Weight loss compared favorably to those of any other controlled study, with subjects in the couples training group averaging nearly thirty pounds lost after eight and one-half months of treatment. In the absence of spouse training, subjects with cooperative spouses (group 2) did no better than subjects with noncooperative spouses (group 3). The findings suggest that spouse-training may have a potent facilitative affect in weight reduction, and this affect may promote long-term maintenance of weight loss.

This study also offers more surprising findings:

1. Husbands were seven times more likely

than their weight-reducing wives to initiate food-relevant topics of conversation.

2. Husbands were almost four times more likely than their wives to offer food to the spouse.

3. Wives were slightly over twice as likely as their husbands to reject food offers.

4. Husbands were over twelve times as likely to offer criticism of their wife's eating behavior than they were to praise it.

Another study done in 1972 by two doctors named Stuart and Davis maintains that some husbands ". . . are not only contributors to their wives' efforts to lose weight, but they may actually exert a negative influence."

The study revealed that there are four things a husband can do for his wife who is wanting to lose weight:

1. Become acquainted with the principles of behavioral weight-reduction treatments. In other words, for those husbands who have wives in Free To Be Thin classes, study the material, go to the classes, keep a calorie sheet of your own for a while to understand what she is doing.

2. Stop criticizing her weight and eating behavior.

3. Learn how to reinforce improved eating habits.

4. Learn how to assist her attempts to re-

structure the conditions and consequences of eating.

Phrases from Scripture begin to make more
sense in light of such a study:

Husbands, love your wives . . .
. . . gave himself up for her . . .
. . . *present her to himself* . . .
. . . husbands ought to love their
wives
as their own bodies . . .

. . . no one ever hated his own body, but
he *feeds and cares for it* . . . just as Christ does
the church.

. . . each one of you also must love his wife
as he loves himself . . .

Also from 1 Peter 3:7:

Husbands . . . be considerate as you live with
your wives, and treat them with respect as the
weaker partner and as heirs with you of the
gracious gift of life, so that nothing will hinder your prayers.

WHEN YOU HELP YOUR WIFE, YOU
HELP YOURSELF!

From verse 8:

live in harmony
be sympathetic
love
be compassionate
be humble . . .

The message from the Word of God, husbands, is not only to be sympathetic, loving, compassionate, and humble, but also *be involved.*

Blessings on you,

Because of Jesus.

NOTES

1. Kelly D. Brownell, Carol L. Heckerman, Robert J. Westlake, Steven C. Hayes and Peter M. Monti, *Behav. Res. and Therapy*, Vol. 16, "The Effect of Couples Training and Partner Co-operativeness in the Behavorial Treatment of Obesity,"(Pergamon Press, Ltd., 1978), pp. 323, 333.

Bibliography

Betzer, Dan. "Putting the Past in the Past," *The Pentecostal Evangel*, December 1982.

Glasser, William. *Reality Therapy*. New York: Harper & Row Publishers, 1965.

Seamonds, David. *Putting Away Childish Things*. Wheaton, Ill.: Victor Books, 1982.

Simons, Sidney. *Negative Criticism*. Argus, 1978.

Slater, Michael. *Stretcher Bearers*. Ventura, Cal.: Regal Books, 1985.

Welch, Reuben. *We Really Do Need Each Other*. Grand Rapids, Mich.: Zondervan Publishing House, 1982.